Jade Sarson

What's important in life?
According to Marie's dad...
INN
There's my little Holy Mary...
It's nativities...

...and, er...
bread that tastes like
sweaty cardboard...

HYMN
BOOK

...and dreary hymns on Sundays.

Those aren't such bad things, I suppose.

Sometimes her mum
says what's important...
...is a cheeky present before Christmas.
Or—
Oh.
Well, it's definitely not THAT.
It's about
marriage,
family...!
Not this—
BLASPHEMY!

They're very...

specific about that.

It's a bit confusing.

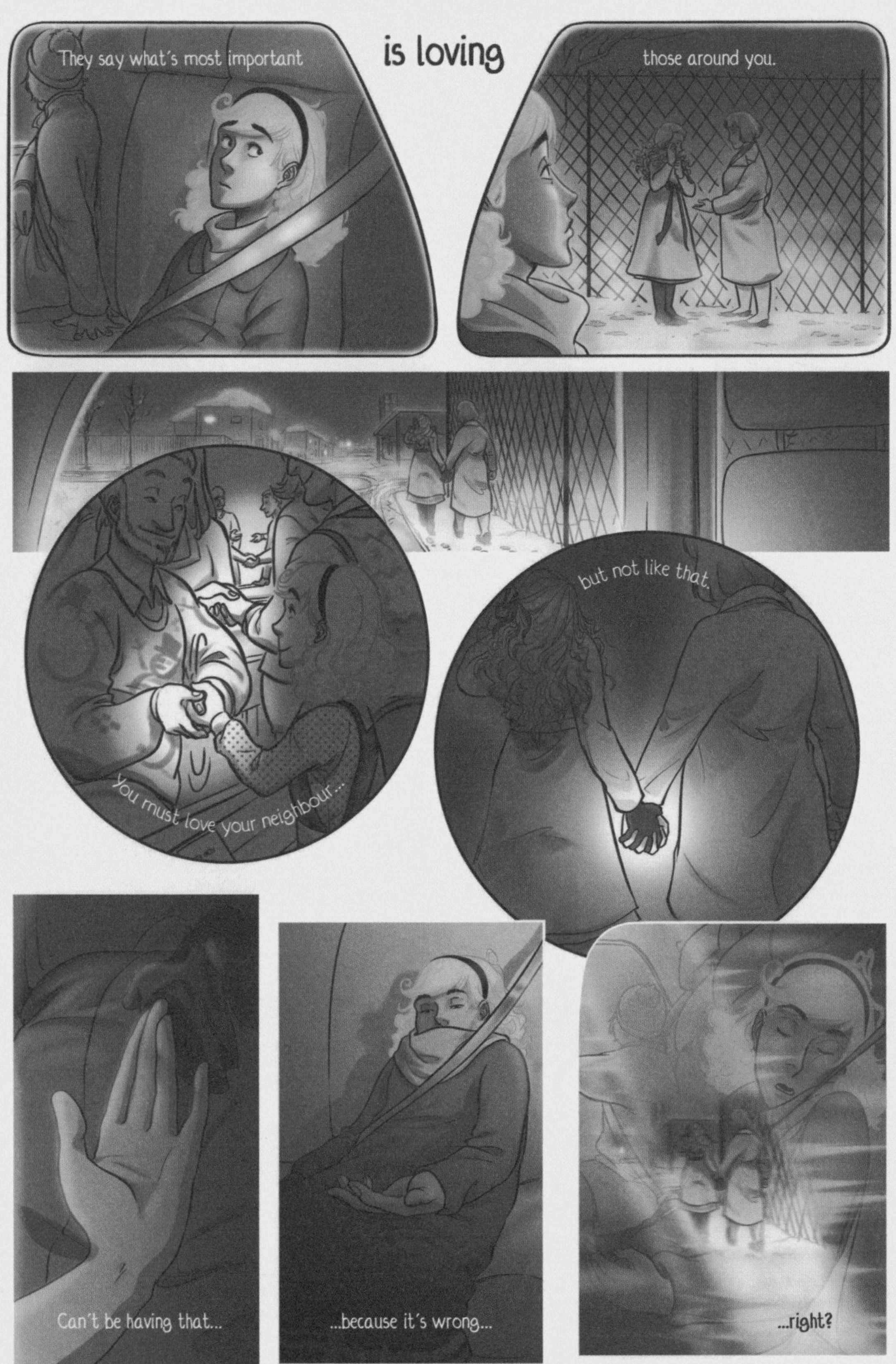
They say what's most important
is loving
those around you.
You must love your neighbour...
but not like that.
Can't be having that...
...because it's wrong...
...right?

For the Love of God, Marie!

Jade Sarson

First published in 2016 by

Myriad Editions
59 Lansdowne Place
Brighton BN3 1FL, UK

www.myriadeditions.com

This edition published in 2016

1 3 5 7 9 10 8 6 4 2

A CIP catalogue record for this book is available from the British Library.

ISBN: 978-1-908434-77-7
E-ISBN: 978-1-908434-78-4

Printed by Pozkal in Poland
on paper sourced from
sustainable forests.

This is Marie.
Excuse the hair, she's had a long night.
Mmmmm.

TOKYO 19
bruussssh
pat?
pat...
pat.
puuuulll
pop!
shuffle
yank!
...
You can't stay in there all day, Colin.
Uuugghhhhhh

Oh yes I can.
No, you can't.

Yes, I—MMPH!

I wish I could stay here all day with you.
Well, you can't. Now. Get. OUT!

Alriiiight, alriiiiight.

Last night was fun, Marie...
Thank you.

See you later?

Yeah.

Alright, *cripple*?

Leave him alone, Johnny.
Go on, Colin
Whatever.
Marie was a very special girl.

She loved to learn.
HEMISTRY
MRS. PUWOLB
Curie was of the opinion that 'Nothing in life is to be feared, it is only to be understood'.
Marie, Year 7
She loved to understand.
You must love one another as God has loved you.
I can see you sleeping, Mister Johnson
blah blah blah
Marie, Year 9
And she loved to LOVE.
Please copy down the diagram and add the correct labels for the male and female reproductive organs.
She had a kind soul, dedicated to understanding people.
...
ew!
haha!
Unfortunately, most people misunderstood *her*.
Marie, Year 11

Even her family have trouble most of the time.
...and their son is missing an arm, did you know?
How awful for his mother to be burdened with a child like that. We should pray for her.
Enough about that. How was school today, dear?
Oh, I learnt that we should love everyone as God has loved us—
That's lovely, dear.
—by *making love* to them!
OH MY GOODNESS!
Dear Lord, what are they teaching you kids in school these days?!
?
CLATTER
?
B-be quiet and finish your dinner.
Marie's mission to love and understand everyone, as she would soon come to learn, would always be misunderstood.

Hey!
Marie is now in Year 13
giggle
giggle
giggle
wave
wave
Poke!
and people still don't understand her.
. . .

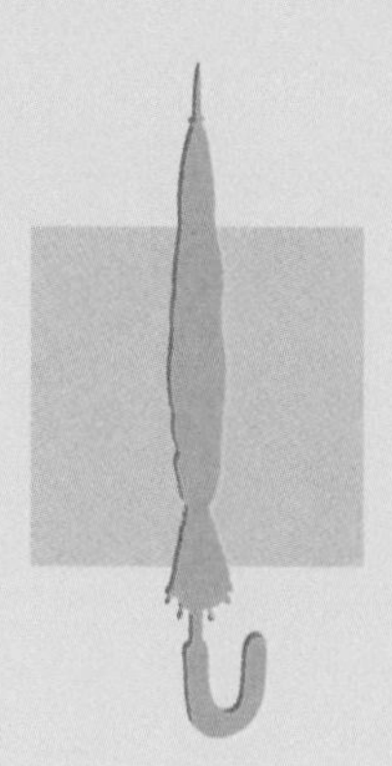

For the Love of Agnes

Oi, Willy!

Willyyy, you big willy—
My name is William.

Why don't you get some balls, Willy!

FUCK. OFF.
Oooooooooooohhhhh!

William.
hee

Please stop disrupting my class.

heh
?
Francis, face the front.

step
step
step
William?
MY NAME IS WILLIAM!
Oh.
That's what you said, wasn't it?
Are you alright?
Not really.
Do you want to talk about it?
Definitely not really.
...
Munch
munch
munch
Is it true you slept with Colin?
Where did THAT come from?

Everyone's been saying—wait, so, it isn't true?
Oh no, it's true.
I'm not ashamed of it, if you are about to accuse me of that.
NO
NO
NO
NO
It's not that...
Marie, don't you think it's weird? His arm, I mean? Aren't you at all... grossed out?
?
No...

ha...

ahahaha!

I'm sorry,
this really isn't
about Colin at all.
It's just...
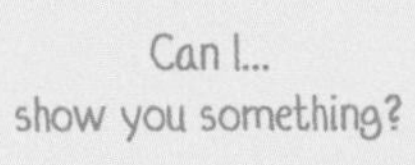
Can I...
show you something?

No one has PE this
period, so no one should come
into the changing rooms.

gulp!

What did you
want to show me?

HUG

Is this what all this was about? You think people will find this gross? How can they?

Don't laugh at me.

You're so pretty!

sniff

I'm not.

What are you do—?
William.
You should just be yourself.
If this makes you happy, then I'm happy for you.
Wait, what about Colin? Aren't you two...?
No, we aren't together.
But—
Do you want this?
gulp!
God, yes.

AH!
ah
ah
?
You deserve love, William.
Everyone does.
Ohhhhh, God!
MARIE?!

In all my years teaching, I have never...
...EVER...
seen such an indecent display of sinful conduct!
I don't even want you to try to explain yourselves—
I doubt you could!
Until we can fix what is clearly wrong with you,
you are both SUSPENDED.
William, we will have to arrange a meeting with your father...
I'm very disappointed in you both.

Oi.
Your, uh,
weird friend is outside.

H-hullo.
Hello.
Gosh, William, I'm really sorry about what happened with the teacher...
I—
I'M IN LOVE WITH YOU, MARIE!

...No, you're not.
But, Marie—
Those things you said to me...
...Were things I absolutely meant.
You deserve to be loved, William.
You really do.
I was the first to accept who you really are but...
I'm not your special someone.
Am I?
So.
This is what happened with Colin?
Yep.

You are...
an amazing person, Marie.
Will you be alright? Your dad...
He can learn to love me as I am, right?
I deserve that.
See you at school?
Yeah.
Poofs.

A few days later, Marie was allowed back into sixth form.
Ohh my gawwd.
There she is!
WHAT.
A.
SLUT!
Excuse me.
What, you got a problem?
Um... what *is* a SLUT?
Marie, would you come into my office for a moment?
AHAHAHA
HAHAHAHAHAHA

Marie, you've got to understand that when your peers call you names you can't take them to heart.
'Sticks and stones' and whatnot.
Miss...
MRS. ANDERSON

What *is* a slut?
You don't—?

A slut is a... derogatory term, or insult, for a... well, a **promiscuous woman,** Marie.

In other words, someone who has sex with many partners.
Why on earth is that a bad thing, Miss?
Because—

Especially when you **love** those people?
Well—

And besides, **sex is really, *really* fun!**
MARIE!

It just doesn't work like that, Marie.
Boys will be boys, you know.
Wait, my brother brings home girls all the time.
I've never heard *him* called a slut!
Marie?
HAPEL

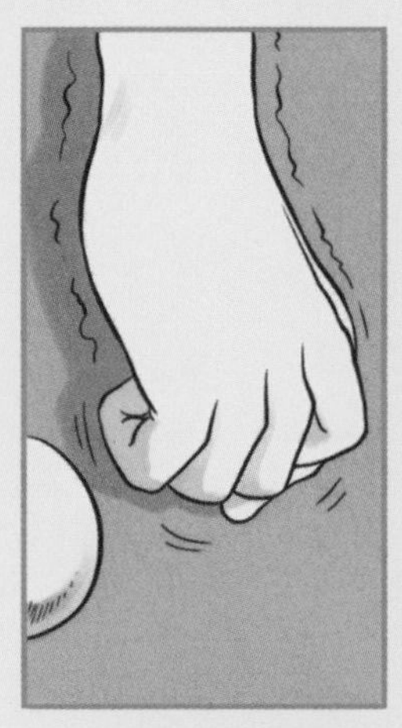

gasp!

sob
hic
sob
hic
sob
mmph

Um...
Oh gosh, I'm so sorry!

D-don't pay any attention to me.
I didn't think anyone else was in here!
It's okay, really, I didn't mean to bother you.

You're...
You're that girl in my class!
Er, yeah, I'm Marie.
You're always sat near the door, aren't you?

...
If you don't mind me asking,
why are you crying?
I-I FELL
You didn't really fall.
Did you?

I, uh, didn't expect to find anyone else in here either.
That's why I came in, actually.
It's funny, for a Catholic school, you'd think there'd be more people making time to pray!
....
Sorry, what was your name again?
You didn't say earlier.
I can just call you 'Chapel Girl' if you like.
But then that makes you sound like some sort of crime-fighting nun...
HA!
My name is Agnes.

Marie and Agnes sat in the chapel for a good long while.
They were missing English, but who cared.
They were probably just reading Macbeth again.
Is this, uhh, a dagger I see before me?
Zzz
Agnes Ratti was being abused at home.
She didn't say it in so many words, but Marie got the gist.
She liked the chapel. No one asked her what was wrong, or about *that*, here.
Apart from me.
whap.
Yes, apart from you!
No one but God was there to judge her.
But why would God judge you? You haven't done anything wrong—
Yes, I have! And if anyone found out they'd call me a...
...Well, a...
What they've been calling *me*.
nod

Agnes... You're not a slut, for God's sake.
You and I have done nothing wrong.
If someone's hurting you, you need to tell someone!
I AM!
I came in here to tell GOD!
To beg for his forgiveness!
Ask for his help!
But I—
I don't th-think—
anyone's eve—
—even LISTENING!
I'm listening.

The weeks that followed were possibly the best weeks of Marie's life.
She sat closer to Agnes in class.
llllllleeeeeeeeeeeesssssssssbooooooooooooosssssssssss
Oho, room in your minge party for one more?
Agnes followed her to the chapel
OW!
BUMP
and there they spent
every
single
break
CLATTER
mm!
shhh
heehee
snogging.

Marie was giddily happy in love.
And then me dad chucked Mum's shoes at me!
Joke's on him, I kept 'em.
Anyway, I think it's time we settled the debate.
Oh not this again.
What debate?
William seems to think The Beatles are the best thing since sliced bread.
Because they are.
Aren't they?
NOO! Elvis is the clear winner.
Beatles!
Elvis!
Beatles!
Elvis!
I'm more of a Stones man myself.
Beatles!
Come on, Ratty, you're the tiebreaker.
Who do you prefer?
Um, I guess The Beatles?
snap!
HA!
Ughhhh.
I GUEEESSSS I still love you.
...
But like all the best things in life...

giggle
heehee
mm!
mmm
mmph
haha
mm
...it couldn't last for ever.
Do you want to stop?
Absolutely—
NOT!
Hah!
I love you, you know that?
...

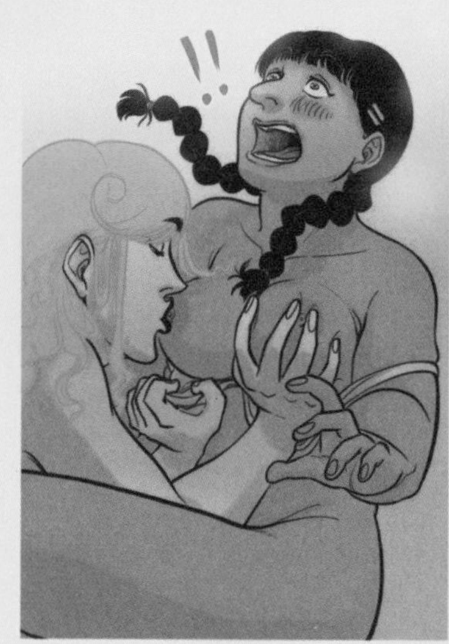
!!

M-Mah—
Marieee—eeheehee!
Oi!
Sorry! It just tickles...
Yeah?

Well...
I bet THIS'LL tickle even more!

Ah!

Ahahaha—
AHHHHHH!

MARIE!
!!

Marie, I expected this of you, but now you've corrupted Agnes?
How can you be so sinful?!
The two of you are suspended for the week, and we'll have to put you in separate classes.
You are not to tell ANYONE that this happened. UNDERSTOOD?
My goodness, you two are disgraceful!
You should be ASHAMED OF YOURSELVES!
How can you be so cruel?
You punish us for loving each other yet you fail to notice how much pain she's had to go through to be happy?!
How can you sit there and—

Marie, please DON'T!
'I don't think anyone's listening...'
'I'm listening.'
WHAT is going on?
YOU ARE SUSPENDED FOR THE WEEK, REMEMBER!
elcome
St MARY'S
AN CATHOLIC
SCHOOL
I'm gonna sort this out myself!
I'll tell her good-for-nothing family to go—
to HELL!

I've never
even...
Nee 
NAW
nee
naw...
woof!
woof
woof
...asked
her where
she lives!

A week later.
It was fun, babe.
Why can't she be more like her brother?
He has... ***healthier*** interests!
Coloured interests, mind.
SHUT.
flick

Not still sulking, are ya?
rip rip
rrrrriiip
You know all these weird friends of yours aren't worth it, right?
Yes, they are!
And they aren't weird.
You're the weird one. You don't even love the girls you're sleeping with!
Of, of course!
You're not, though, are you, Miss High-and-Mighty?
We're not so different.
It's alright to, y'know, have a bit of fun.
But you need to grow a pair if you're gonna get away with it like I do.
grab
You sure about that?
YES!
And you DO?
flick!

NO, IT'S NOT ALRIGHT!
I let Agnes down.
I thought I could love her, understand her needs, but in the end, I...
I was selfish and took everything I could get from her, instead of saving her from that god-awful family.
I'm like YOU. There, you happy?!
I'm a terrible person!
No you're not.
You're not a terrible person.

You're a wonderful person.
Um...
I—
TSSSSSS
Wait!
Read the letter, o-okay?

Soooooo.
You gonna read that or what?
Dear Marie,
I'm sorry I didn't tell you all this in person, but you know me. It's hard to talk about this stuff.

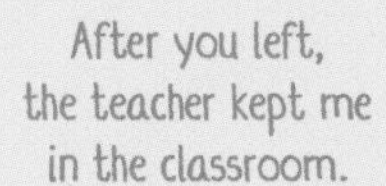
After you left, the teacher kept me in the classroom.

I think after your outburst she knew something was wrong.

I told her I didn't want to go home.
It was scary but eventually I had to tell her why.

It wasn't as bad as I thought it would be,
and I think I had the courage to do it because of you, Marie.
Because if you listened to me, maybe they would too.

The good news is: I'm finally free of my family - I don't ever have to go back home!
The bad news is: I can't stay here, either.

The teacher took me to Father Dreary,
who decided it would be best if I lived under care for a while.

I'll be going to work in a laundry in London tomorrow,
where I'll stay until I'm ready to live on my own (or so they say).

I can't be with you anymore,
but at least I'll be away from my family.

I might never see you again,
and I'm not nearly brave enough to say this in person.
So a letter will have to do.
I love you, Marie.
Thank you for listening to me when no one else would.

love, Agnes x
I, er...
I was joking about the whole 'Miss-High-and-Mighty' stuff.
I'm sorry.
No you weren't.
No you're not.
You *really* love her, don't you?
Oh, William!
Who the heck is William?
I found MY special someone!

And right when I found her, I lost her!
Ahhh, c'mere.
So...
You're into chubby chasing, huh? No wonder you're upset!
There there
You twa-ha-haaaat!
Sob!

paf.
Staaa
arrrre
fling!
fwp
bruuussssh
PULL
love, Agnes x
SLAM!

Your vest's on backwards.
I know.
And inside out.
No socks either!
Heard you the first time.
Honestly!
SPORT
The MOON
Can't you even make yourself look presentable, young lady?

BASH

SLAM

HA!
HA!
HAHAHA

I wondered when she'd drop the cute act.
Looks like she's finally growing up.

...and your final exam will be on the 12th.
I want you all to stick to your revision schedules.
And try not to get caught up in any unsavoury distractions.
RRRRIIIIIIIIIINNNNNNG!
!
C-class dismissed!
Y'alright?
...
Wanna come back to mine with me and Colin?
Why not?
Urgh!
Let's get a wiggle on then, I need to get outta this uniform.

That's better.
Very nice.
I don't think I've ever seen you in short sleeves before, mate. Look at those biceps!
It used to bother me, I guess.
I wore long sleeves all the time to cover this up.
But...
I honestly don't give a shit anymore!
Miss Millner tried to get me to change earlier...
...but fuck that!
Haha yeah!
Now.
Lookie what I got 'ere!

Only the finest borrowed Irish piss for my fellow school-leavers!
COUGH
Wait...
Is this your first drink, Marie?
COUGH COUGH
COUGH
What do—
ACK!
—you think?
COUGH
Hahaaa, you're adorable!
gulp!

Just one more—
Hic!
—month and we're free.
No more b-bloody nuns.
No more Maaassss.
No more of that bollocks.
Just straight up boxing for meee.
Well...
...without the straight part, in my case.
Wait, I thought you and Marie...?
Oh, we did.
But I've always fancied blokes. Like you.
Whuh—?
I guess that means you're the only woman I'll ever love, Marie!
Awww.
cheers
H-how fuckin'— sweeeeeeeeet.
Oh my God, Marie, you're so drunk! I've never heard you swear!
Heeheeheeeeeee.
Heeee.
I feel loads better.

Careful...
I'm sooooo done with being a student.
I've decided.
easy!
I'm gonna—
I'm gonna be a, a teacher!
So... you're leaving school...
...just to rush back in?
......yep!
Alright then!
oof!
To the boxer, the teacher an'...
er, what are you gonna do, Colin?
I'm... off to a uni in Scotland, actually.
Got my acceptance letter the other day.
...Oh.
Yeah.

Well then!
ahem

To the beautiful boxer, the sexy teacher and our new Scotsman 'ere!
clink!
'Raaaaaaayyy
The torture of attending Catholic school ended for them in June of '65.
But a new torture was in store.

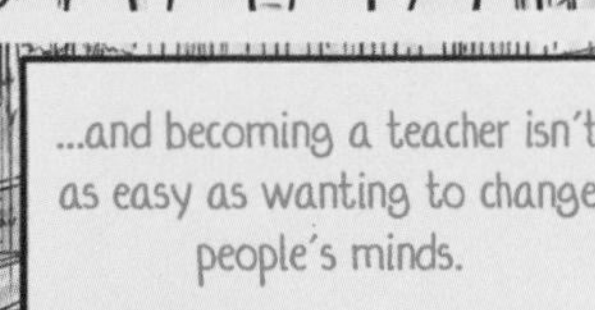
al express
Because, God knows, becoming a boxer isn't as easy as wanting to punch people...
...and becoming a teacher isn't as easy as wanting to change people's minds.

And then there were two.
Bugger...

BAY 3
BAY 2
BUS
I forgot my umbrella.

For the Love of PRANNATH

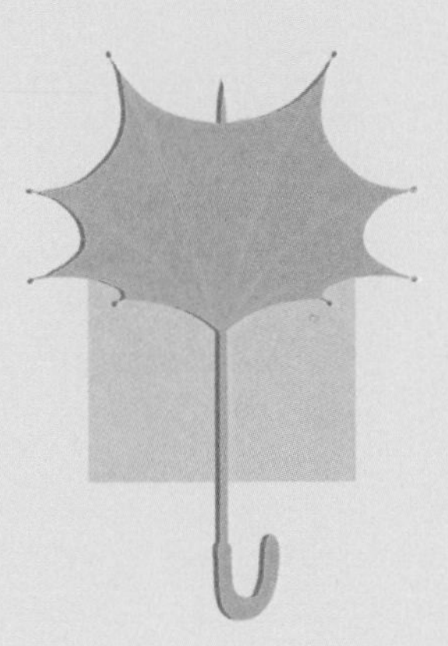

Shit, shit...
I'm going to be late!
Language!
Sorry!
For God's sake...
...can't you behave more like a lady?
Bite
munch munch munch
munch munch munch munch munch
gulp.
You're right.
...that was exactly what I needed to hear.
What was I thinking? On my first day of teacher training college, of course...
KICK!
These heels are MUCH more LADYLIKE!
BYE!
SLAM!

Marie had been hoping for at least a 'good luck' from her parents.
But that wasn't important.
...Not now that she is on her way to her first teaching class.
Not now that she has shifts to do at the working men's club later.
And only a few hours until she has to return home, to her parents...
hwooooooooo
...who didn't wish her good luck.
plip!
Oh!

Bugger!
I forgot my—
Umbrella?

It was a long first day for Marie.
Mmmmph.
Welcome to the W.M.C.
DARTS COMPETITION THURSDAY NIGHT
W.C.
'Allo, love, are you an angel?
Because you look heavenly!
What. Can. I. Get. You?
Oh! William, I thought you were...
Only taking the piss! Bad first day?
Wow.
W.C.
Lemme get changed and I'll walk you back. You can tell me all about it, alright?
SIGH.

...and THEN he said I should wear something like one of the other girls!
I thought I was there to study!
Not for him to look at my legs!
What a prick!
...and can you believe the nerve?
He suggested I should stick to the Primary course instead of Secondary!
What's the point of going if I get the piss taken outta me for asking a bloody question!
Now, now, I'm sure it'll get better once you settle in.

I've been meaning to ask, what's with the umbrella?
You've been fiddling with it all the way back!
That's just about the only nice thing that's happened to me today.
It started to rain on my way through the park, and I'd forgotten my umbrella.
This bloke just up and gave me his!
This umbrella man...
...was he, ah, dishy?
Why'd you ask?
Because I haven't seen you smile like that since...
Er, nothing, never mind—
Agnes.
S-sooo, what's he like, when are you seeing him again?
Oh, I don't know, Will, he was just some bloke I bumped into! I'll probably never see him again!
See who?

Speakin' of seein'...
...are you seein' anyone, love?
Because I am free as a bird right now.
heeheehe
What?
Not your type or summat?
Oh, mate,
you couldn't handle my type.
flick!
Hahaha. Come on, Johnny.
?

You won't need that, it's not gonna rain today!
She doesn't know why she took the umbrella with her, really.
It's not like he'll be there again.
People don't just wait around for you to—
Hello again!

Won't you join me?
I didn't know there were chess tables here...
There aren't.
This is mine.
Care for a match?
You mean you brought...?
Er, no, sorry, I can't. I have a class to get to.
By my watch, the college doesn't start classes for another 50 minutes. Plenty of time.
I, uh, don't know how to play though...
That's alright, I'll teach you!
This is called a pawn...
Stay.
Please?
!!

Aaand that's called a checkmate.
I win.
Ugh!
My apologies, I didn't mean to so thoroughly trounce you.
Gosh, it's later than I thought.
Oh really?
Sorry to have kept you.
Blimey, I better be going!
I better not be late because you had to show off!
Don't worry.
I'm sure your teacher will forgive you.

Leg it!
Leg it!
LEG IIIT!

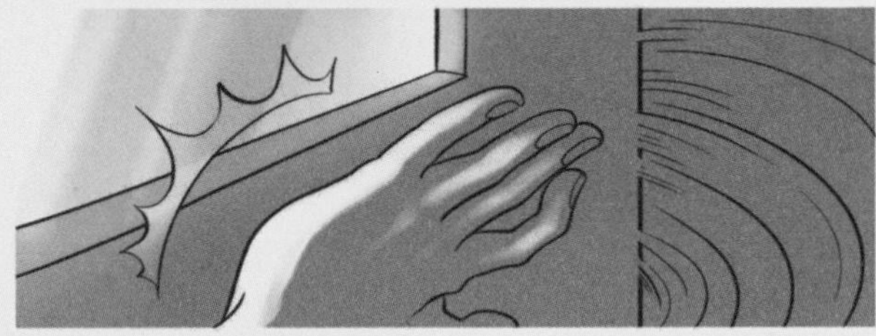

S-sorry, I got held up, am I late?

You interrupted me introducing the Secondary modules teacher! Go and sit down!
Now, now...

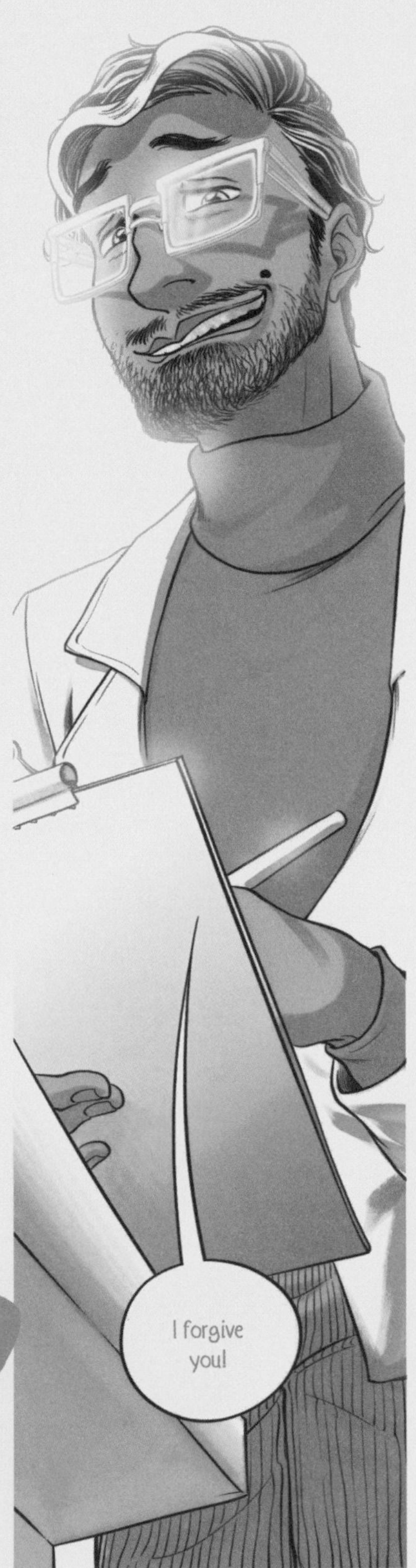
I forgive you!

It's alright.

Ms Lovitt?
You've been glaring for a while now.
. . .
sigh.
Why didn't you tell me?
lean

I wanted to live in the illusion for a little bit.

What illusion?

The one in which I get my umbrella back!
Oh gosh, that's right,
I meant to,
earlier that is...
I—

Tell you what.
If you win, you can have it back.
Oho, that should be simple enough!
And if I win, what do I get?
You?
Why, you get to keep it, of course!

Checkmate.
...I think.
Well now! You're a fast learner!
I have to be going, my shift starts in a few.
!
heh.
Thanks for the umbrella!
Now just wait a moment!
I demand the opportunity to win it back!
Oh my, you think you can?

I know I can.
I challenge you, Ms Lovitt. Will you be available for a rematch tomorrow? Say, 4pm?

You know I will be...
That's right after my afternoon class, Professor Dubashi.
Mister Dubashi...

Let me live in the illusion a little longer.

—rie...
Marieee...
Marie!
S-sorry, Will, I was miles away!
Oh, didn't you have time to change after your match?
Umbrella Man?
nod nod
We are NOT talking about my boring arse match.
(Which I won, of course.)
I can change later. Right now, I am walking you home and you are going to tell me everything!

BOOOOOoooooOOOOOoooOoooy
hell.
No wonder you looked like you'd had a stiff one.
THAP!
Will!
What? Really, he sounds lovely. Y'think he'd do it in his tweed jacket?
Would you stop?
RUMMAGE RUMMAGE...
He doesn't even have a—
Ohh no.
Whassamatter?
I forgot my keys.
56
So? Just knock!
Mmrrrrmmmm.
Maybe I can just climb the drainpipe...

When you are QUITE finished drawing attention to yourself on my doorstep...
...would you like to come in?
No one is looking, Dad.
Indeed.
And who are you, young man?
Me?
Er, I'm Will, sir. William Cummins.
My dad runs the boxing club next to the workin' men's.
Mmhmm.
I suppose that explains the shorts.
Well, thank you for walking my daughter home, Mr Cummins.
Goodnight.
Er, yeah, goodnight, sir.
Alright, Johnny?
?
You coming in or what?
Nahh... couldn't be.

Marie didn't forget
her keys again after
that little fuss.
Mr Dubashi won
back his umbrella
the next day.
He let her try
to win it back
again the day
after that.

And the next day...

...and the next.
!
Until they forgot who actually owned it anymore.

Sorry
I'm late,
my final class
ran over a bit.
But I don't have
a shift today so we
can run over too!
I'm sorry,
the what?
Smell that?
sniff sniff
I didn't
know it had
a name
already.
Well, it
didn't until
a couple of
years ago.
Wait, I
wouldn't.
Ahh, I hate it
when that happens,
leaves nowhere to
sit!
splish!
Then let's
walk.
We can
take in the
petrichor.
That's
petrichor.
Ohhh.
sniff sniff
ahh
There was
a fascinating
scientific journal
that—

NGH!
TWINGE
Are you alright?!
Y-yes, yes I'm fine.
Wait, you said 'already'?
I had another name for that smell before.
I think I prefer it to be honest.
And what was it, pray tell?
Well...
I met you in the rain, so...
Prannath.
You said you're free tonight?
Yeah, why?
Do you fancy coming back to mine?

It's spitting.

Maybe I should go.

touch

I want a rematch afterwards.

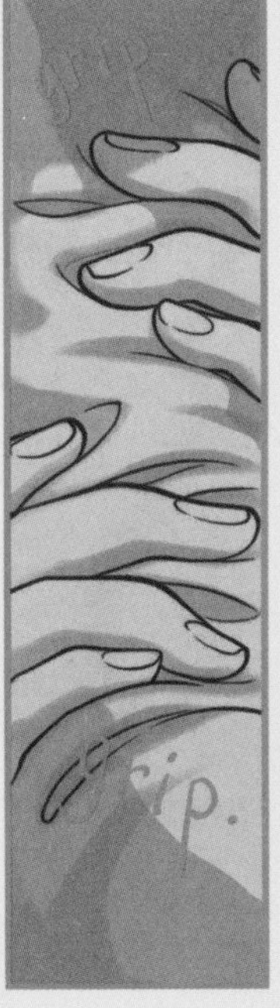

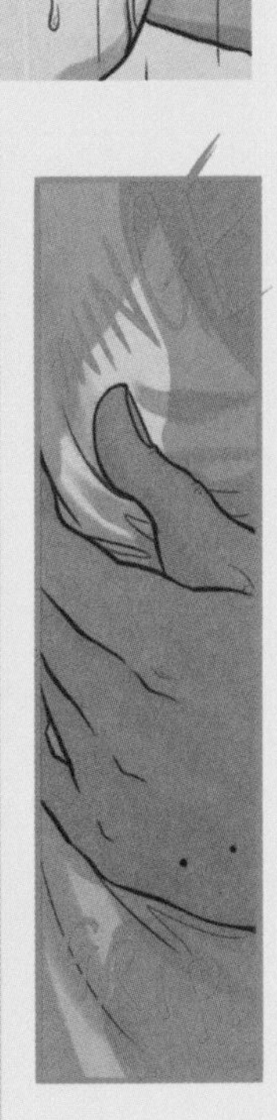

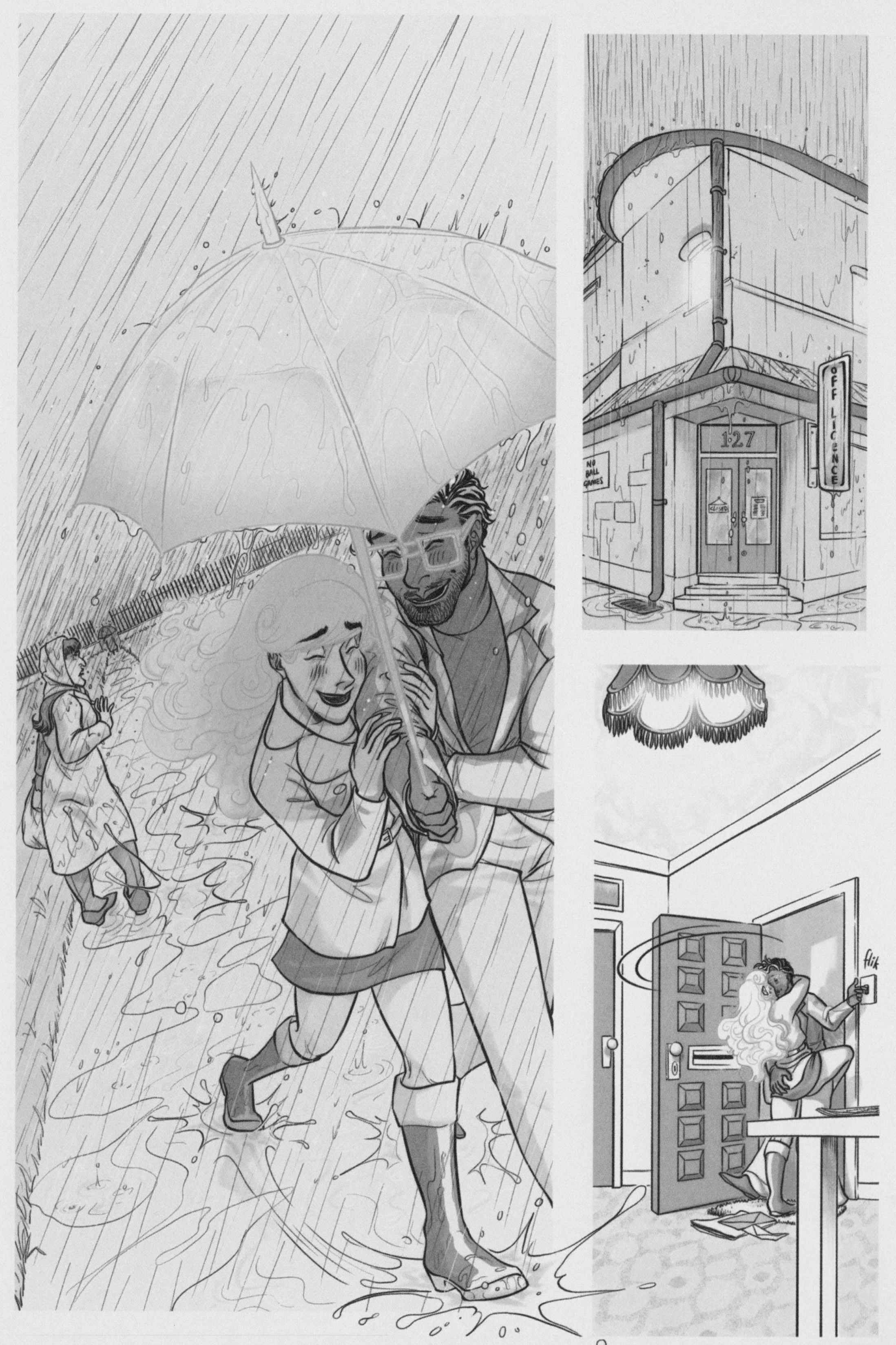

OFF LICENCE
127
NO BALL GAMES
CLOSED
flik

We can...
...stop.
We don't have to...
No,
no, no.
No.
Okay.

HmmMmmmMmMmmmMMmmMmMMMmm
Your mother picked an awful name for you, now that I think about it.
Whaaat?!

What makes you say that?
Well...
'Marie' in some languages means...
'Sea of Bitterness'.
Check.
Huff.
Mum told me I was named after Holy Mary, Mother of God...
Well, I wouldn't know much about that, seeing as I believe in Hindu gods...
Hm.
But I wouldn't worry about it, Marie.
For all it matters, your name to me right now means
'Sea of Ecstasy'.

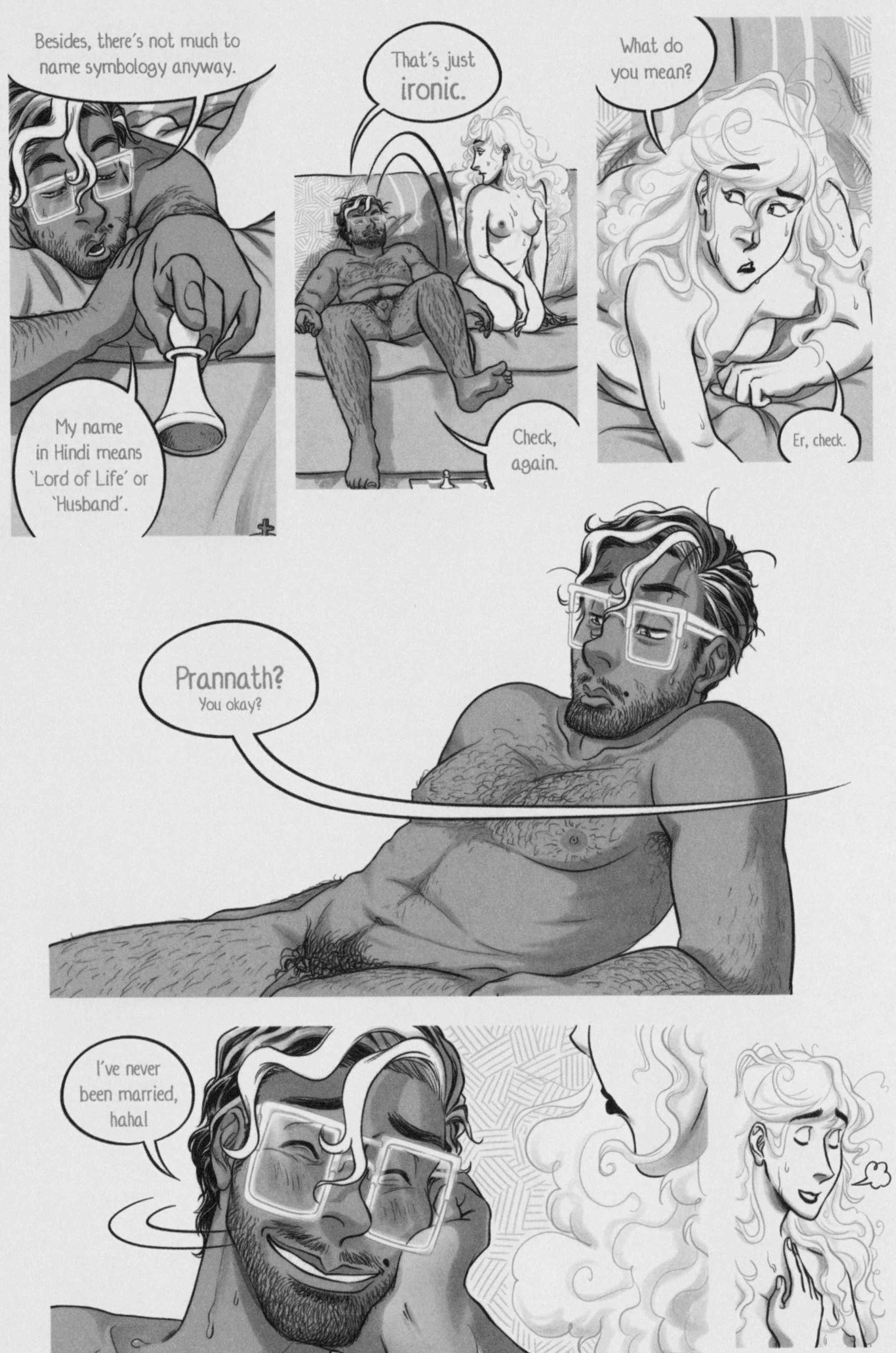
Besides, there's not much to name symbology anyway.
My name in Hindi means 'Lord of Life' or 'Husband'.
That's just ironic.
Check, again.
What do you mean?
Er, check.
Prannath? You okay?
I've never been married, haha!

Well,
you could always...
I dunno...
marry me...
I s'pose.
Your turn.
Oh!
CHECKMATE!
I WIN!
Alas! Claim your prize.

Marie had noticed that a lot of people have trouble saying what they mean.
For example, Prannath said:
Oof.
That umbrella's quite cold.
When what he wanted to say...
more than anything...
...was yes.

Marie...
I'm afraid our rematch will have to wait.
It's time I gave you...
...a right.
Good.
ROGERING.
HA! hee hee hee

click!
Oh, hi Mum.
And—
Aunty Pat?
Oh! So! You recognise me NOW do you?
I beg your pardon?
!
Your aunt saw you yesterday.
Out gallivanting with some Paki twat?!
He—
He's Indian, actually.
WHERE HAVE YOU BEEN ALL NIGHT?
Dad, I—!

WITH HIM?!
Dad, STOP!
FOR FUCK'S SAKE!
I don't understand, Maureen.
What did we do to deserve
such a disgusting
WHORE of a daughter?!
It's not your fault, David!
Heeeey, look who I found outside!
Dad, I-I didn't mean—
Marie—?
!
...What the fuck is going on?
Marie?

Why couldn't you just be NORMAL?
Why do you insist on upsetting us like this?!
You never used to do this!
I didn't mean to!
Please tell me you aren't thinking of marrying that scum.
Can't you marry a nice English boy?
Like that Cummins lad...
I don't even care if he's Church of England, he'd be better than that uncivilised—
Marie isn't doing ANYTHING she doesn't want to.
And neither am I!
YOU CALL YOURSELF HER FATHER?! YOU BIGOT!
C-C-CUMMINS?!

TH-
THUMP

AGH!
David?!
EURGH!

Come on, Marie. Let's go.

But—
Ugh—!
JUST GO!
For God's sake, Johnny, PHONE AN AMBULANCE!

ING CLUB
Sorry
I haven't been to the shops,
we've only got digestives...
BLESS THIS HOUSE
Ugh, they're not even chocolate.
S'alright.
CRUNCH
nibble
nibble
Why is it...
always
about THEM?!
Because people are cocks.
Ppbfft.
No really!
It's always gonna be about them.
I don't put dresses on to upset my dad but that's still how he sees it.
Shit, look!
I even made this pep talk about me!

Come live with me.
Will...
Dad's gonna let me have the flat at the back. We can split the rent.
It'll be fab...
Will you at least think about it?
I appreciate it, really...
Oh!
Maybe Prannath will let me move in with HIM!
I should call and tell him what's happened.
Umbrella Man?

Hm, he's not picking up.

Marie...
Sorry, Will.
I'll be back later, I just...
I need to go and find him right now, okay?

I'll be here when you get back.

shut.

I'll always be here.

SNAP!

Mmph.

Classes are finished for the summer.
He's not at home.
He's not in the park.
the look on them kraut faces when we win!
Something pulls her feet in the direction of his flat.
KNOCK KNOCK KNOCK
Even though she knows he isn't there.

Hee heh We did iiiiiit.
30 July 1966 was a busy day indeed.

BUMP!
Oi, cheer up, love! We won!
Give us a smile!

ENGUHLUUUUUNND!
ENGUHLUUN

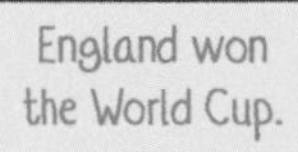
England won the World Cup.

Suit yourself, ugly cunt!

Prannath Dubashi died.

And later that night,
KNOCK
KNOCK
KNOCK
so did Marie's father.

In accordance with Hindu customs,
Prannath was cremated.
Marie wasn't
invited.
She was, however,
begrudgingly invited
to her father's funeral.
Murmur
...my father...
Murmur
whisper
...brilliant
man...
Murmur
Murmur
whisper
whisper
...miss him...
whisper
...goodbye,
Dad.
Would David's
daughter like to
say a few words
as well?

My father and I didn't always get on.
Understatement.
He was...
PAKI* TWAT!
s-supportive, but he was also...
WHORE
...a...
There's my little Holy Mary in her tea towel!
...a good and decent man.

Did you hear?
—tacky glassware.
Mm, heart attack.
—and he was wearing a dress?!
Anyone know where the loo—?
—has always been strange—
Poor Maureen.
ah
ahhh

MARIE?!

Marie, it's not what you—

Please, don't tell any—
It's alright.

I know.
This is what you need right now.
I...
understand.

Wow, she's as weird as Betty said she was.

Maureen?
'The funeral is on Thursday...'

I expect you to be there.
It's the least you could do.

Seeing as it's your fault he's dead.
I—
Of course I will, but... Wait Mum, please!

I know you didn't like me being with Prannath.
I know.
But I've lost someone too and... I've lost BOTH of them and I...

I really need you right now—
I'm so...

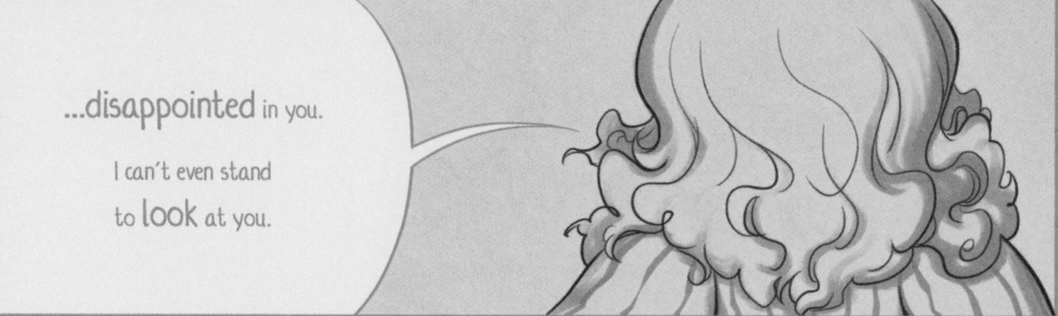
...disappointed in you.
I can't even stand to look at you.

Thursday. Don't be late.

Mum—!

God help me!
Er, are we still gonna...?

glug

Tell me...
what do you see?

I see summat I'll be banging later once I've finished this.

I see.
And there?

Hmmm.

A dish like that I'd have wiiiiith...
red wine. Mmmm.

I see two people who desperately need a push in the right direction.

Away from you.
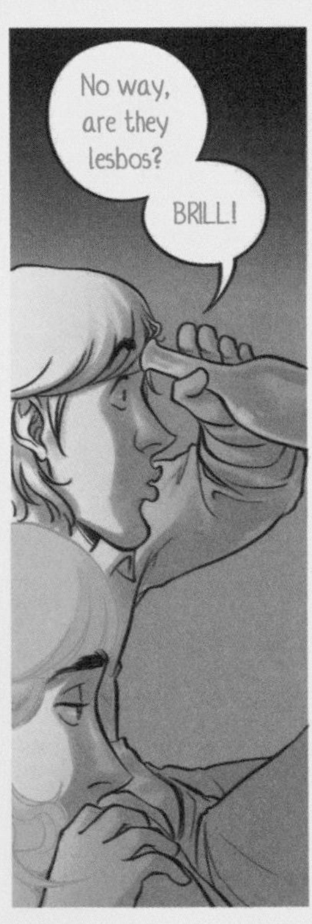
No way, are they lesbos?
BRILL!

Awwright, ladieeeeees!

Aw, there they go...

Do you know why Dad loved you more than me?

I'm more handsome?

I dunno.
Maybe if you'd been more ...normal?
He just wanted what was best for ya.
Marry some nice bloke.
Give him some grandkids.
Y'know, normal stuff.
Debatable.
Who is white and doesn't cross dress.
...

Well, I'm halfway there.
Hm?

Nothing.
Don't stay out here too long, y'might catch cold.

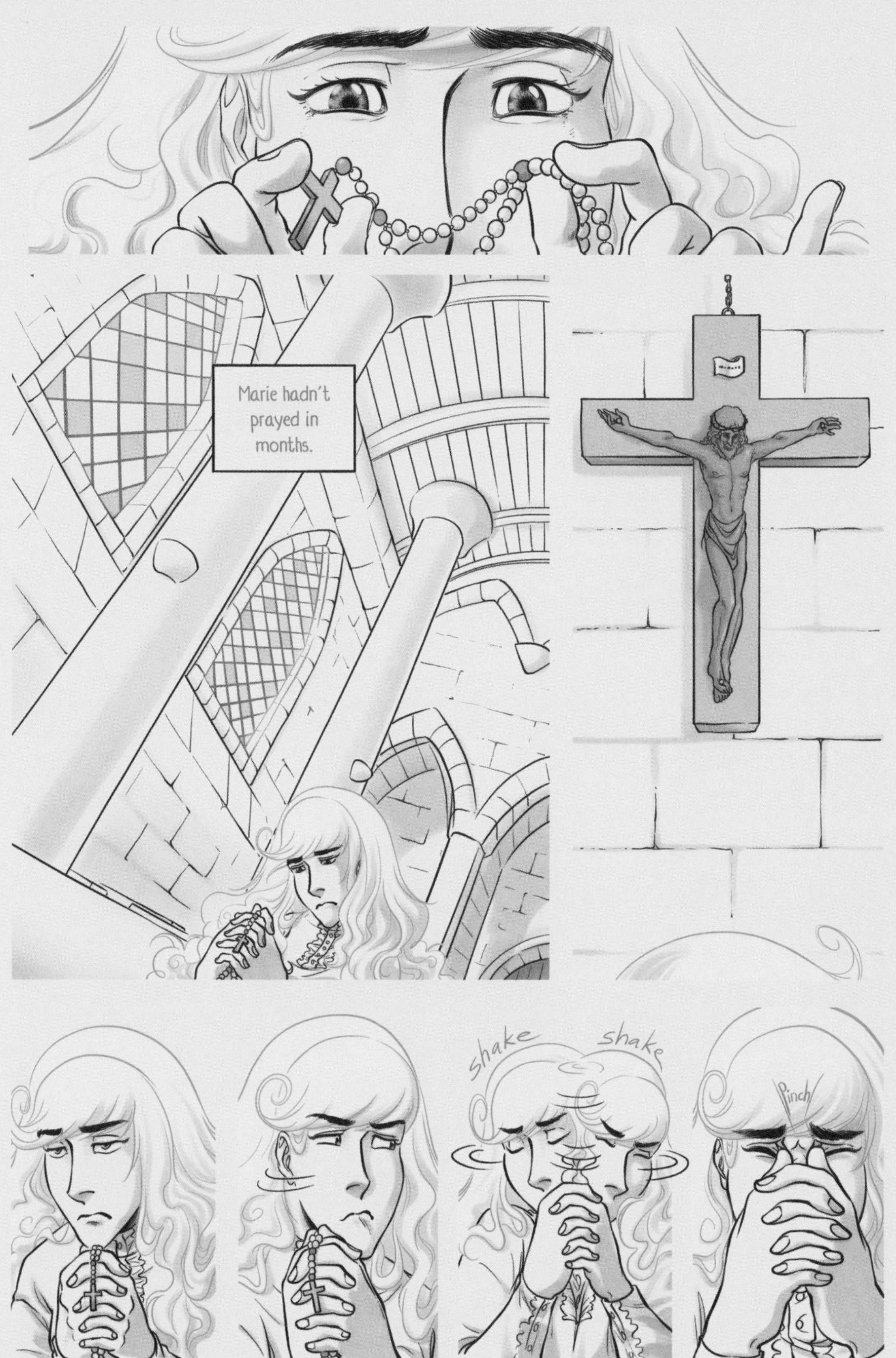
Marie hadn't prayed in months.
shake
shake
Pinch

Are you punishing me?
Is that it?
If you are...
don't you think it's a bit much?
I thought I understood what you wanted from me.
You told me to love, so I loved!
Did I do it wrong?
Did I love the wrong people?
I just don't understand!
I don't understand...

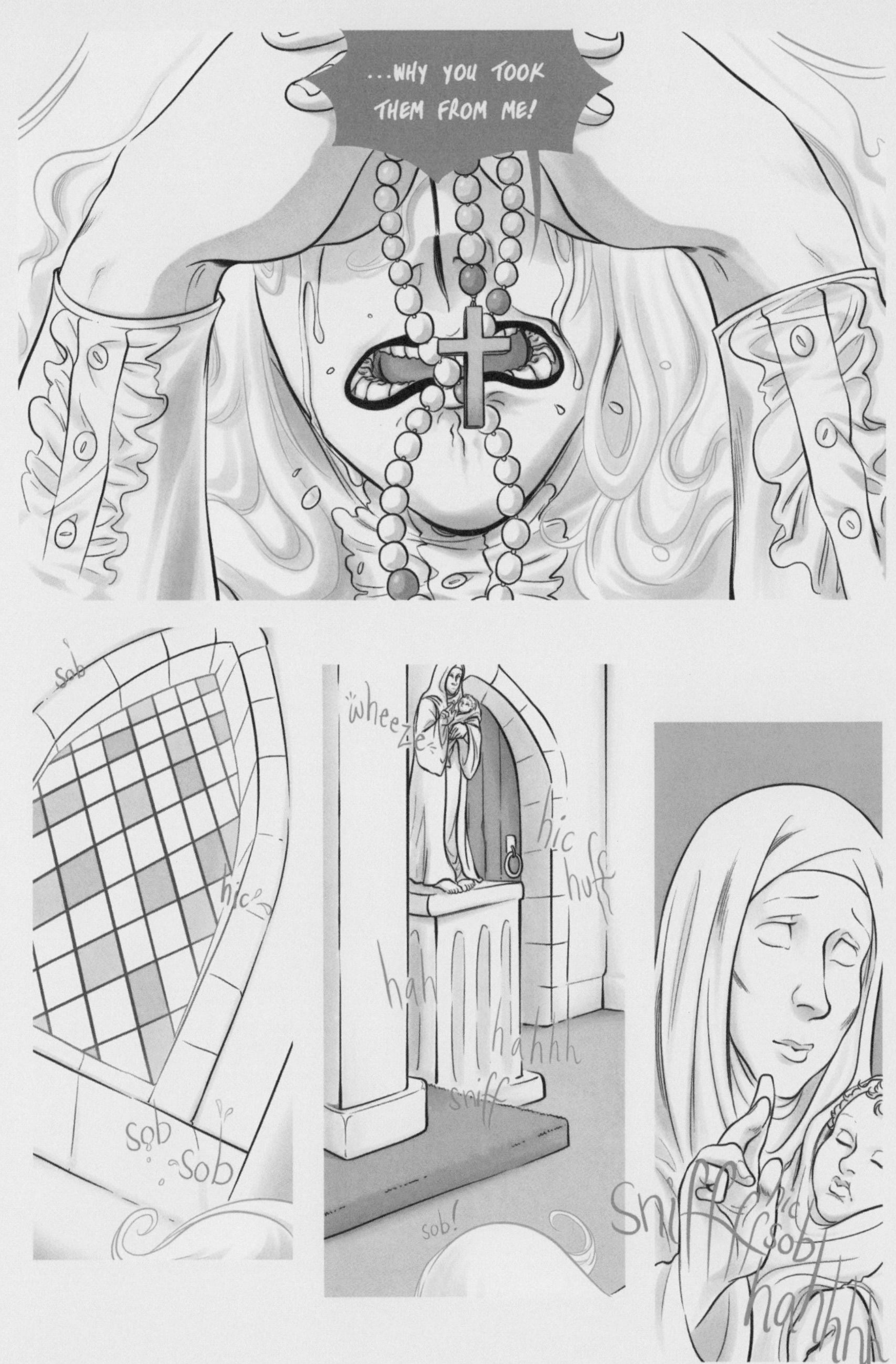
...WHY YOU TOOK THEM FROM ME!
sob
hic
sob
sob
wheeze
hic
huff
hah
hahhh
sniff
sob!
sniff
sob
hah

hhh
I'm done listening to you. And...
sniff
I'm done talking.
Oh!
David's daughter, right?
Are you alright, my child?

Rrrumblllle
KELLY
JENKINS
1902–1955
CARING
SISTER
Plip
Hah,
bugger,
I forgot
my—

You look
like shit.

Come on.
Let's go
home.

According to Annie, Marie and William always say they can't remember most of 1967.
It was a long year.
They moved into the second flat above the boxing club together...
CHEERS!
...got pissed.
WINNAAARRR
CHAMPION
William won a major local final,
and they got pissed.
five minutes left!
Marie nearly failed her teaching course, but managed to scrape a pass,
and, naturally, they got pissed.
They shagged a few people...
...shagged each other...
(They definitely don't remember that, they were very clear about that.)

Oh, and she gave birth.
They might've been pissed WHILE she gave birth.
This is Annie, by the way.
Funny how terrifying a little wailing blob can be.
Abortion was legal by then
and Annie's still surprised...
...her mother hadn't even given it a second thought.

For the Love of annie

She grew out of wailing, eventually.
This is Annie aged 11.

Excuse the hair.

Z Z Z Z
Someone kept her up all night.

tink
tink
tinkle
tink
tinktink TINK!
Uuurrrghhh...
Shhhhhhit!
I'm gonna be late!
I thought you didn't have work until later.
Oh! Morning, darling.
That's right...
but I've got an interview first thing!
TA-DA
Oh. Well, good luck, I suppose.
Be good while I'm gone, darling.

SLAM!
whuh
Er, hullo.
...'lo.
!
Phwoooooo!
WHAM!
What a niiiiiiight.
Alright, poppet?
Oho!
So she DID bring you home.

Go on then, what's up with you?
You wot?
What's your 'thing'? Marie only spends time with...
mm....
interesting people.
It's kind of what she does.
There's, uh, nothing...
Should we be discussing this in front of...?
SSSP
We're gonna start guessing in a minute.
Maybe it's **brain** damage?
NO.
No, it's not that.
...

I was just...
really angry yesterday.
Lookin' for a punch up,
you know?

But then she
showed up at the
bar and...
I didn't feel
like hitting
anyone.

Ahhh. How
nice for you.
Well,
that's our
game over.
You can go
now.
SHOO
SHOO.

Er, right,
yeah, nice...
meetin' you.

CLICK.
Nanny says
picking your nose
isn't ladylike.
Yeahhh, well,
Nanny Lovitt
can go to—
clink!

Ahem.
You didn't answer
me earlier -
are you alright,
poppet?

NO, I'M NOT ALRIGHT!
Nanny said Mum's going to Hell.
She said people who do things at night with people who aren't married...
go to HELL!
Mum always says it's okay to love people and...
and do THOSE things with them but I don't...
I don't want her to go to Hell!
Nanny said...
Hey, hey, heyyyy, come on now, shhh shhh shhh.
sob sob SOB

I knew it was a bad idea letting her look after you last week...
Was she lying?
Your nanny just likes to make people feel bad, poppet. Don't pay it any mind.
But she s-said...
What did she say, Annie?
Sh-she said I'M bad too...
because Mum didn't baptise me.
OH FOR F—!
You listen to me now, okay?
You are the sweetest
sniff
smartest
most adorable GOOD little girl in the world.
And your nanny is a very... lonely old lady.

But—
Your mum didn't baptise you because she didn't want to force you into something when you were a baby - when you couldn't say no.
That's what Nanny did. Your mum loves you too much to force anything on you.

Alright?

If she loves me sooo much...

Why aren't I enough for her?!
Annie...
No! Why does she have to bring home strangers to love...

...instead of ME?!

Annie!

SLAM!

Your mum does love you, Annie.
Please believe me.

Listen, I'm sorry, poppet, but I've got to get ready for training.

I'll be downstairs if you need me, alright, poppet?

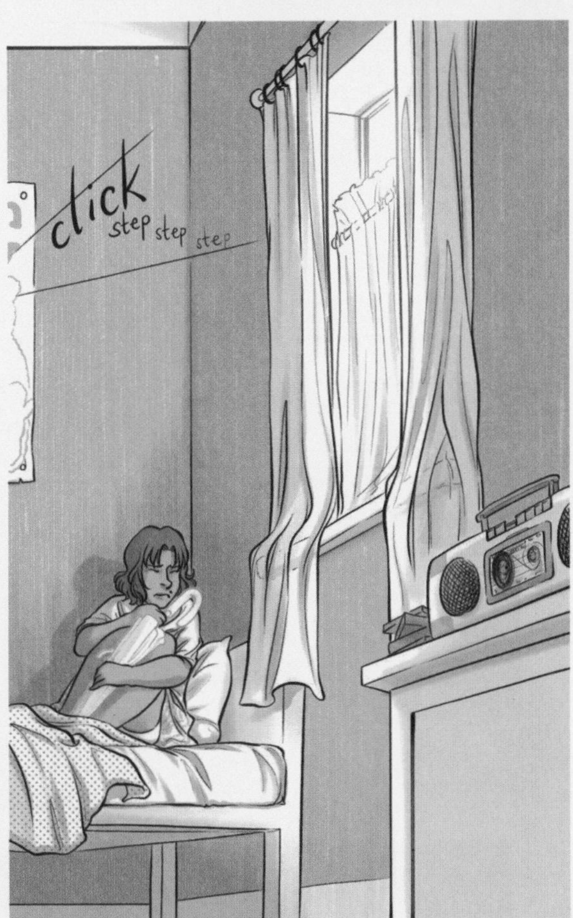
click
step step step

Same again, please, luv.
W.C.

Whassamatter, luv?
Got the painters in or summat?

She wants to quit.
Ah, come on, don' be like that.

You can talk to ol' Bill.

Sigh...
I had an interview for a teaching job this morning, and it, uh... it didn't go so well.

Oh dear. Thassa shame, love.
But chin up, eh?

No one wants a sad pair of tits at the bar, yeah?

She REALLY wants to quit.

BOXING
squeak!
LUB
W.M.C
RULES!
`Ere, son, I want you t'meet our new heavyweight.
Herbert Pluta.
Call me Bert.
He's gigantic!
I know!
Awwright, Bert.
Cor, nice big strong hands!
Stop teasin' 'im.
Oh, he's a good'n!
Oh!
Who's the bird?
M-Marie!
Hey!

Hm?
What's got your knickers in a twist?
Oh I swear—

If ONE more pillock
mentions my knickers
OR my tits, I am going to THROW SOMETHING!

Blimey alright, I was only asking.
Sorry.
It's just my interview went...

Well, it went shit, alright?
I was doing well until they asked me
what my HUSBAND thought of me working in a school.

When I told them I don't HAVE a husband...

...they decided they didn't like me as much as they thought.

Shit.
Quite.
Then some old fart decided to mess me about in the club,
and to top it all off...

What?
Will...

It's...
it's the
30th.
Ohh—
oh fuck,
already?
Shit -
I'm sorry, it
slipped my
mind.
It's alright.
I was tempted
to go and check
on Mum,
actually—
OHHH
NO!
No way, José!
I am not letting
you subject yourself
to that today.
We are going out,
and we are going
to cheer you the
fuck up!
I dunno...
GRUMBLE
Uh, how
about some
food, first?
BLE X CROSS X X
Are you
sure your
dad's alright
looking after
Annie?
Yeahhhh,
they'll be
fiiiine!
Come on.
Let's get
sloshed!

12 years.
You'd think that'd be enough t-time to—
to—
BRRRRP.

But noo, here I am, STILL getting fucking depressed.
Why can't they just leave me -hic!- aloooone?

What do you mean? Are they haunting you?

Noo, you arse, I just mean...
sometimes I look, y'know, and I see them. I see them telling me I fucked up.

You haven't fucked up.
Did... Did Annie seem quiet- quieter than USUAL at dinner?

Oi, do you know something?!

Hey, look, is that Bert?
Who the fuck is Bert?

He's the new heavyweight, didn't I tell you?

I didn't think he was...
Rise
Hey, I'm gonna go say hello.

Er, I don't need you to come with me—
Don't panic, I'm not.

I'm going home. I wanna see Annie.
Oh, alright. Are you sure you don't wanna...
Nah.

But you have fun with Bert.

Hello there.
...touch...

Hullo yourself.

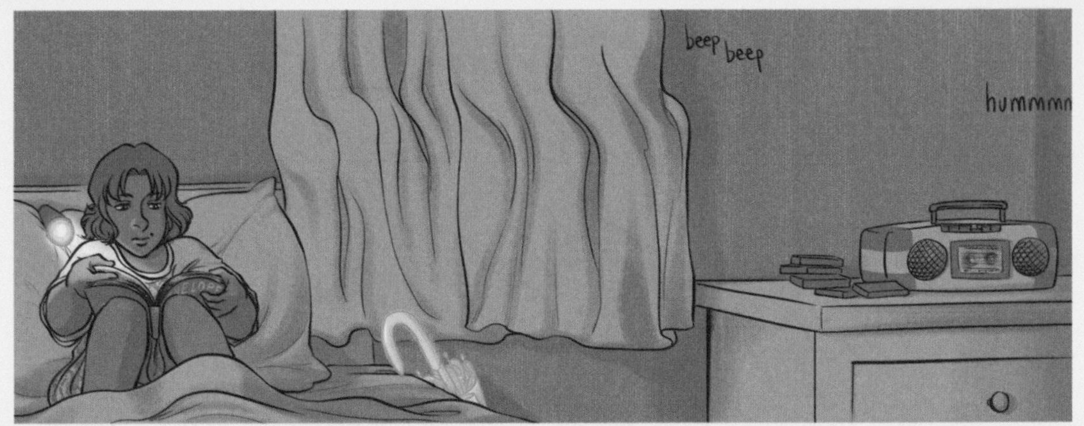
beep beep
hummmm

click!
Thanks, Ricky.
clatter
oomph!
No, no, I'm alright.

Yeah, thanks for looking after her.
'night!

SHUT.
click
click

tmp
tmp
tmp
owwww
BASH

KNOCK
KNOCK
KNOCK.

Annie?
Are you a-awake sweet-hic-heart?

Mum...?

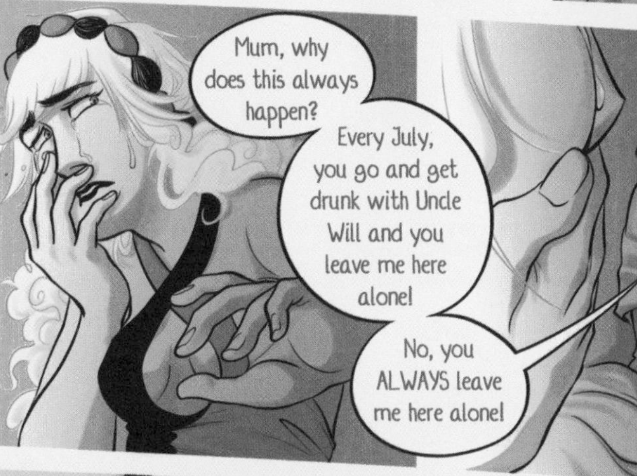
Mum, why does this always happen?
Every July, you go and get drunk with Uncle Will and you leave me here alone!
No, you ALWAYS leave me here alone!

I'm sorry...
Is this about my dad?
I'm a big girl now. Can't you talk to me?

I'M SO-HUH-RRYY-yy— hic!— sob—

SHUT

ah!

Nudge...

Smack

Wooo!

FLOP!

You're so fucking beautiful.

Er...
But it's alright 'cause then you sauntered over!

And you're fucking gorgeous, thank God! I really thought...
I didn't go for women anymore!
Listen, Bert...

Thank fuck you came along.
I need to tell— ah, wait!

Wait!

Shh, it's alright, darling, I'm gonna fuck you into next—
ZZZZZZiiip!

—week?

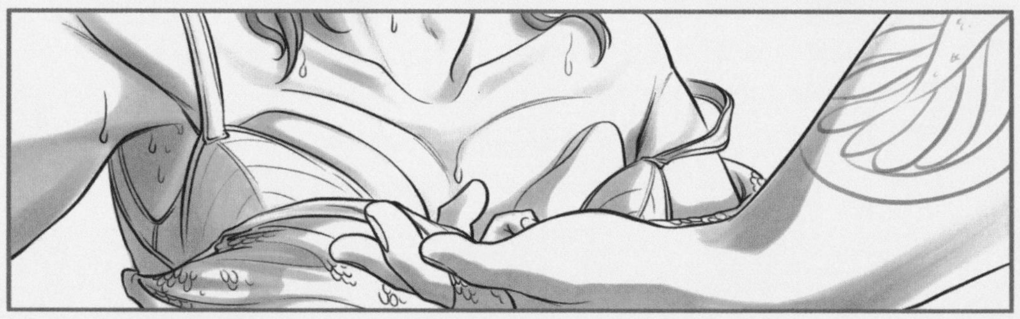

Bert, I...
How do you know my name?
I-it's me! Will! From the boxing club?
I thought you recognised me when I said hello!
How the fuck was I supposed to recognise you?!
THUD
You're wearing a bloody dress, you sick fuck!
Please, Bert, it's alright.
gulp!
Let me explain...
twitch...

Oh my God—
just—
CRASH
GET THE FUCK OUTTA HERE, WILL!
ugh!
step step step
SLAM
YANK
ffffff—
SHIT!

blink
blink
I have to go to work.
Will you be alright on your own?
Kiss...
I've been alright all summer, haven't I?
See you later.
I love you.
Mornin'.
Or rather, afternoon.
Are you alright, son?
What, no cheeky comment?
There's only me 'ere.
Why don'tcha go 'n have a wash? Get something on that chin.
rub
rub
Dad...
!!
CLATTER
BAM.

Pluta.
We're CLOSED
today—
I don't
care.
Oi,
Willy-
Woofter.
Take off
that dress
and put
on your
shorts.
YOU.
ME.
RING.
NOW!
rrrip
This ain't
even a fair
fight...

DING!
Whoa!
Bert—
You don't have to do this.
We can stop.
clench!
RRGH
Oi, don't let aggression mess up your technique, Pluta!
Don't help HIM, help ME!
I'm a coach, what can I say, lad?
STOOOOP—
FUCK YOU!
TRYING TO
MAKE ME

What are you on about?!
YOU GODDAMN FAIRY!
?
Yeah, what IS he on about?
Yeah, that's right!
You can't seduce ME!
Fucking POOF!
Yahhh!
Ugh!
!!
What's going on?
YAH!
oof
ugh
bish
agh!
bash
Isn't that Bert?
bash
Yeah, you know him?
Well no, but last night they were...
uhhhhhhhhhhhhhhhhh...
Ah.
I see.

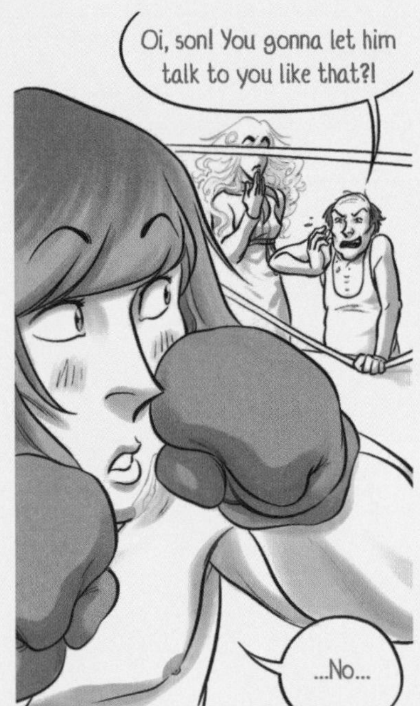
Oi, son! You gonna let him talk to you like that?!
...No...

NO, I'M NOT!

You...
hah...
bloody... pansy...
Come on then, you Willy—

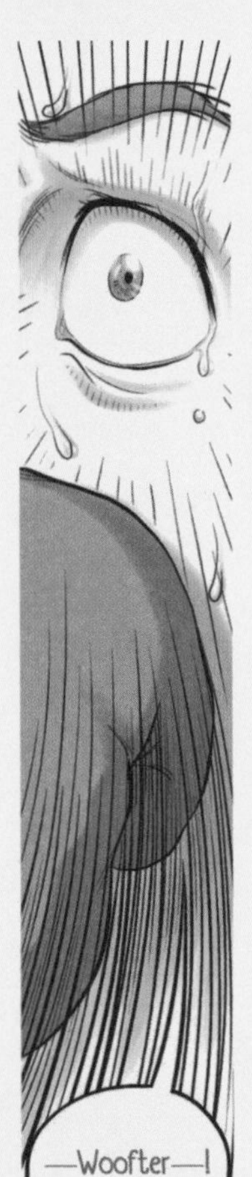
—Woofter—!

Bert...

FUCK OFF!

WHAM

Thassenough, lads. I think you've proven me point.
DING!
'Cause my boy Willy was never gonna lose.
Hiya.
Dinner?
This wasn't a fair fight.
Starving.
I take it it didn't go so well with Bert last night?
What makes you say that?
Oh, I don't know, maybe seeing you deck him just half hour ago?

Did you knock him out, Uncle Will?
Hehe, nearly!
It was in the ring, Annie, so it was okay
but you should never punch people outside a boxing ring.
RIGHT, Uncle Will?
I dunno...
I'd've hit him outside as well if he hadn't run off already.
WILL!
WHAT?!
Violence isn't the best way to deal with problems, okay, sweetheart?
Hey, at least I'm DEALING with my problems.

What is THAT supposed to mean?!
Oh, you know exactly what it means.
Annie, why don't you tell your mum what you told me yesterday, hm?
Um...
You've been neglecting your own daughter! All because you can't get over Umbrella Man.
Come on, Marie.
It was 12 YEARS AGO, for Christ's sake!
How?!
How dare you talk about Prannath like that!
And I lost my dad that day too
or did you conveniently forget what you did?
You still HAVE yours, AND he doesn't have a heart attack when you dress up!
You keep whining about not being able to wear a dress when you box...
...but at least your dad accepts you! Mine can't because he's—
Oh BOO fucking HOO, Marie, your dad's dead, cry me a fucking river.
SMACK!

Annie's room
Annie, go to your room please, I don't want you to hear this.
No! What's Uncle Will talking about? Who is Umbrella Man?
Annie, please—
Ah, go on, tell her, Marie.
Tell her how you shagged your college professor right before...
the shame of it all killed him.
Annie's room
Whoa!
SHUT
Annie's room
FUCK YOU!
She can still hear us.
Then let's take this outside.
Oh, another punch up, is it? COME ON THEN—
SLAP!
What the hell's the matter with you today?!
Are you still drunk?

I'm sorry but I can't just punch all my problems away.
I can't punch away the old gits who leer at me in that shitty club.
I can't punch head teachers into giving me a better job.
I can't punch more pennies into my pay packet.
PUNCH
I have to look after Annie on the little I get.
Oh, but look at you!
You literally live off of punching people!
You must be so fucking proud!
You know what? I AM!
I should be the one taking care of Annie! I'm loads better at it than you!
At least I LISTEN TO HER!

I tell her it's going to be okay when her mum's latest shag hangs around while she eats her breakfast.
I tell her I'll be there for her!

You don't deserve to be her mum!

I should be the one with such a beautiful daughter.

I should be the one who gets people to fall in love with me so easily!

I should be the one...
...who looks so beautiful in that dress!

Ungh—!

Fuck this.
Fuck the lot of you.

Will, where are you going?!
Where do you think?

creeeak
SLAM!
So... this was his then, hm?
My dad's, I mean.
My clever girl.
click!
FWUMP!
Ah— Isn't that unlucky?!
Not with this umbrella.
It's special.
It protected me from... a lot of things.
It kept me company for years.
And I had hoped it would do the same for you.

Annie, this umbrella is the only thing I have of your dad's, and...
it's the reason I have you.
Your dad gave it to me when we first met.
Why didn't you tell me this before? You - you never tell me anything.
I'm sorry Annie, I just...
I'm so afraid.
Of what?
Of telling you the WRONG thing. My mum, my dad, my teachers all told me a lot of wrong things. It's hard to know what's right or wrong sometimes, even for— especially for grown ups.
I just want to be a normal mum for you— but I've no idea how!
I don't want a—
'NORMAL' mum!
It's okay if, if you do it wrong. I just wish you'd try!
I... understand.
I'll try to do better.
I promise.
And that's it from us, now for the local news where you are...

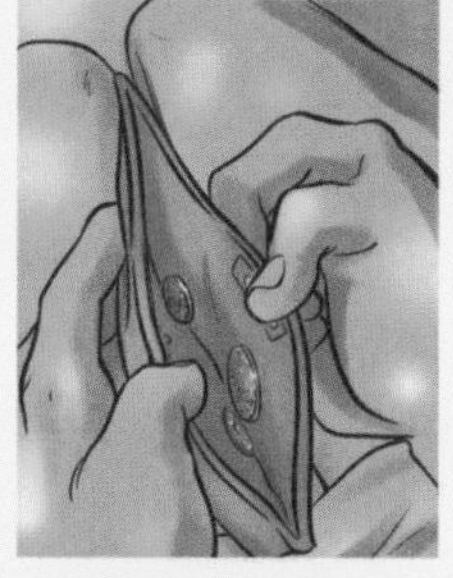

sigh

ft
ft
ft
ft
ft
ft
ft

It'f juft not my day, if it?

Oi, mate, got a fag?

Oh, I forgot!
You ARE one.

Didn't think you'd stoop so low as to hit a beautiful woman, Bert.

Nah.

I wouldn't.

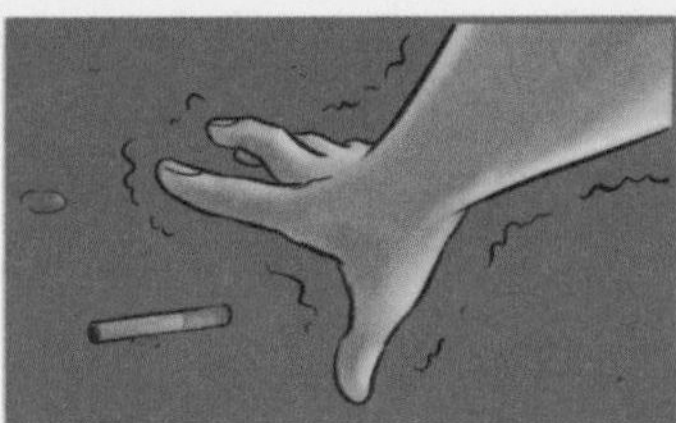

fft
ft
ft

FUCK—!

clatter!

nee
naw
nee
naw...

Mum...?

Do you have another interview tomorrow?
Yeah.
Good - Good luck.

We've just received breaking news—
There has been an explosion at Double Cross, a popular bar in the local gay community.

Firefighters were on the scene just ten minutes ago suppressing the blaze.

Several patrons are reported to be dead or injured,

but we cannot confirm how many...

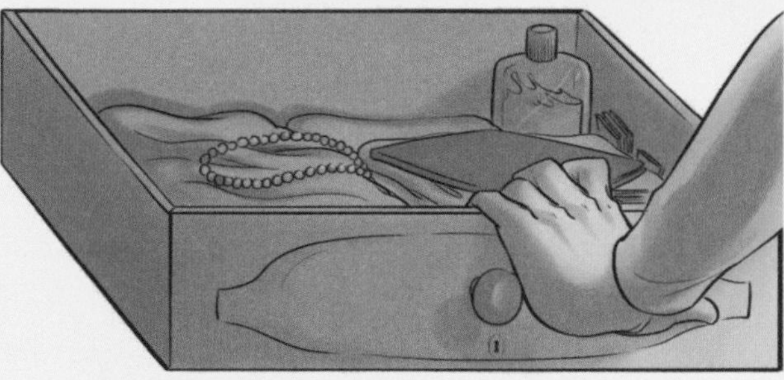

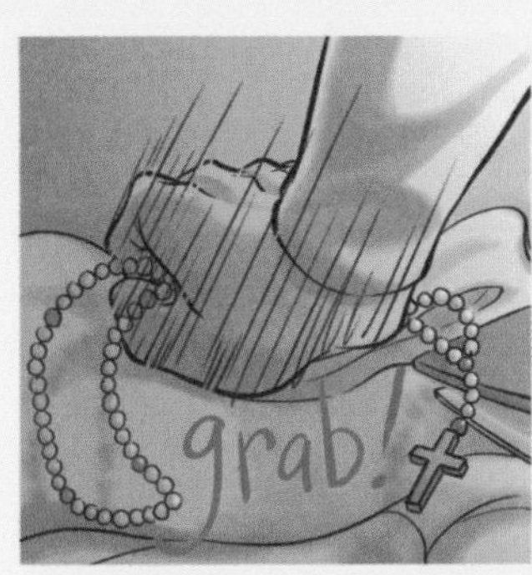
grab!

Marie hadn't prayed in years.

Don't you dare—

DON'T YOU DARE!
Don't...
take my best friend now too!
I'll—
I'LL NEVER
FORGIVE YOU!

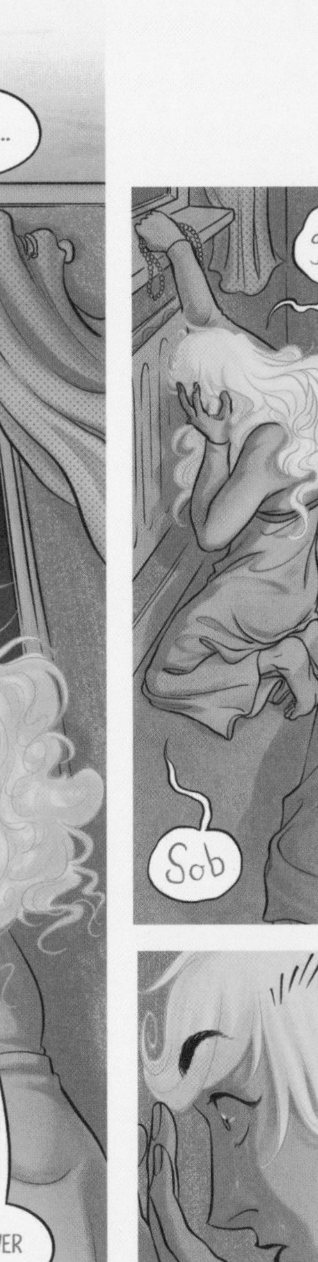
gasp!
Sob

Marie...?

You're alright!
Whuh—? Oh!
You heard then? Yeah, I'm fine.
I was outside.
Marie, I'm so—
SHUT UP.
Shut up, you big idiot!
I really am though.
I know.
Why can't everyone be like YOU, Marie?

...another bombing in a long line of planned attacks on the gay community.
More on this story as it develops.
Now, Chris, what's the weather looking like for us today?
Pbbbphhhhhhhhhhhhhh
Well, Leslie, it's not looking too good for us early risers...
I hope Lola wasn't working last night.
I didn't see her at the bar, but I'm sure if she was...
tug
She... probably got out.
And now it's time to wake up with *The Breakfast Shoooow!*

Why didn't I think of—
that?
MUUUUUM!

Welcome to Class B!
EXTRACURRICULAR ACTIVITIES!!!
SPORT
ART
SCIENCE
THIS WEEK'S
Let me introduce your new form tutor
...
Mrs Lovitt.
THUD.
Well, that was easy.

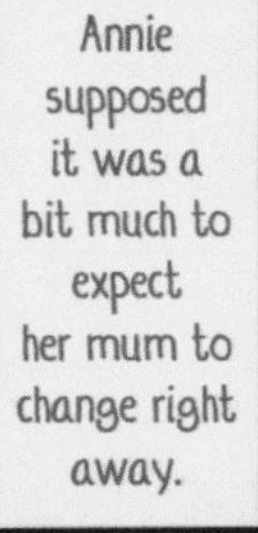

Annie supposed it was a bit much to expect her mum to change right away.

Change takes time.

But eventually her mum started being more honest with her.

Perhaps TOO honest...

When she was 12 and started growing hairier...
itch itch itch
itch itch itch
—and in PE today they just kept teasing me!

Oh, darling. I can show you how to get rid of it...

but don't feel like you have to just because of those girls.

You, my treasure...

...are just fine the way you are!

Aw-awright, just gimme the thing so I can get on with it!

...she wished her mum would stop keeping an eye on her.

When she was 13 and her period started...

lift
blink blink

Ah— AH— AAAAHHHHHHHHHHHH!
!!
MUUUUUUUUUUM?!

Annie?! What's the matter?

AM I DYING?!

pffff
DON'T LAUGH! Go and get the pads from my drawer.

You're not dying.
It's perfectly natural, if a bit of a pain.
You'll just have to wear these once a month—
Every MONTH?
And don't worry about your sheets—
Can't you just give me a book on this or something?

There's no need to be embarrassed—
Okay, j-just get out, I can read the packaging on my own!

I recommend starting with the towels, darling. Tampons can feel a bit unpleasant at first to push up your—
MUM, PLEASE.
...she wished her mum would just stop talking.

When she was 15 and started having strange feelings in her lady bits...
I've been thinking I...
well, that is, I get funny feelings when I, um...
see pretty girls and I...
I think I might like girls.
It'sjustaphaseit'sjustaphaseit'sjustaphaseit'sjustaphaseit'sjustaphaseit's
JUST A PHASE
Oh, that's WONDERFUL!
WILL, GET IN HERE.
Annie thinks she might be a lesbian.
Oh, honey, that's brilliant.
You can come with us to Pride next week!
And I can introduce you to Lorraine, and Louisa, oh and Loretta!
They'll love you!
Wait, do all lesbians have to have L names?
What? No, what makes you say that?
?
Now, lesbian sex is different from straight sex dear, they won't have taught you in school.
Lemme explain what—
Oh, this'll be good!
—and then you—
I changed my mind oh my god please stop
...she wished her mum would leave her alone.

But she'll never leave her alone.
Good morning, class!
class rep
July: Andrea
This first period will be private study.
Because she's still trying to figure her out.
Now, I don't mind if you do something else...
like reading that novel I'm told you are SUPPOSED to have read for Miss Anderson's class later.
Just make sure you're quiet so anyone who is revising can concentrate.
Otherwise, I'll be up here the whole period if anyone needs any help.
I'm not just talking about revision, either.
If you've got any problems you wish to discuss, just come and give me a nudge.
Now, where's the register...

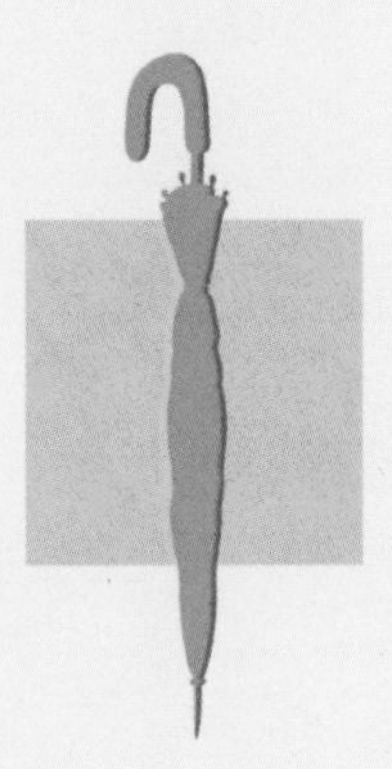

For the
LOVE
of
Marie

Luckily Annie had her own way of escaping.

I've got something Miss Lovitt can help with, if y'know what I'm saying.

Nudge nudge wink wink!

Hey, didn't your dad...?
Yeah, ugh, the bitch. I saw 'em together at the weekend, can't believe it.

I thought you said your dad was lonely?

Well... Well, YEAH, I did, but that don't mean he should— Me mam only fucked off a MONTH ago!

Hey, if Miss Lovitt is easy like that...

imagine what Annie must be like...!
Heh heh heh

Bet she does it like a *Razzle* girl, hehehehe!
Speakin' o' which!

...
giggle
giggle

EVISION
OR

RAZZL

—!

chuckle

When I said this period was for private study...
Hahaha
hahaha
!
!
that DIDN'T mean you should spend the time studying Annie.

AHEM.
Mister Scarpa!

I dunno what you two are laughing at. Don't think I didn't see your magazine.
Hand it over.

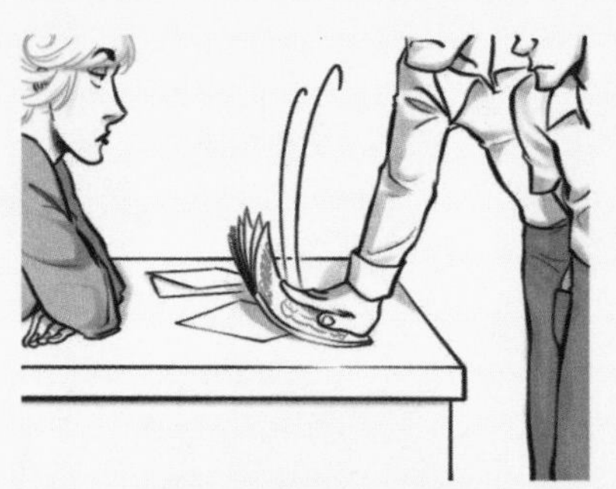

Er, miss—
Well boys, I'm sorry to tell you that most women aren't actually as smooth as Cindy dolls down there.
You might want to study some more...

!
!

HAHAHAAHAHAHA
accurate depictions of female anatomy.

Annie? Where do you think you're going?
To the library. s'quieter there.

I'll get home when I get home, okay?! Just leave me alone.

About dinner later—
I'm going to be late, I want to pick up a new tape at the shops after school.

Oh, but Will's doing your favourite, bolognese!
SHHH!

Rocket Rec
se

BALL
GAMES

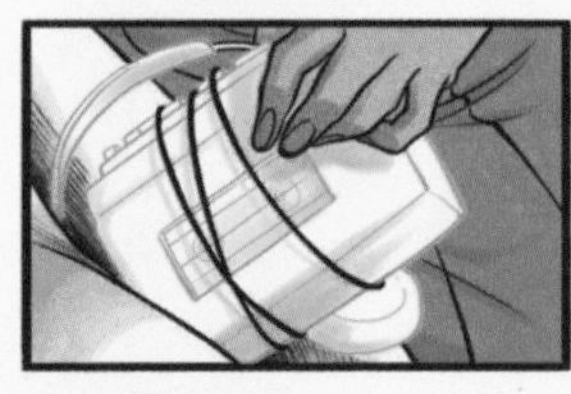

click!

k-thnk.

I can't believe that bitch!
She might as well've lopped my balls off!
Ugh, that WAS horrible.

Oh, it's Annie.

Ehhhh, fancy getting your own back?

Oh, no waaay! Mate, where'd you get THAT?!
Dad's shed.
toss

!
It's only a little'un. Makes a small bang and a flash.
But it should scare the shit out of her!

No— OI, what're you thinking?!

Don't worry, mate, just gonna make her jump, is all! It'll be a laugh!
These things fizzle really loudly, she'll hear it way before it bangs and jump out the way.
Come on, don't be a twat.
Wait—!
chk
fssh
ffff
ffffffff
ffffffffffffffffff
Why isn't she moving?
ffffffffffffffffffff
Oh shit.

Marco, don't!
Oh!
Hello, boys!
Y'know, you didn't come and pick up your magazine after school.
You can have it back now!
Er, thanks, miss.
What's going on?
Er...
ANNIE!
Ohh—
Fuck me—!

GRAB

TOSS

JOLT!!

Mum?!

I told you to leave m—!
OPEN
Pffft.

GAMES
BANG!
FIZZZZZZZZZ
POP

Aw, that was rubbish.
POP
fizzzzle
crackle

What the bloody hell is that racket?!
FIZZZLE
pff
pfft
pfut.

What the heck was that noise?

Why'd you push me over, Mum?!

Can't you EVER leave me alone?!

Sorry, love, I just—
What's WRONG with you?

I just wanted to...
...to...

...protect you.
flinch!
Mum...?
You're my daughter, you know...
I need to—
huff...
take care of you.
Mum, I didn't mean it!
MUM!

Don't
leave me
alone!

touch...

What are you doing?!
!!

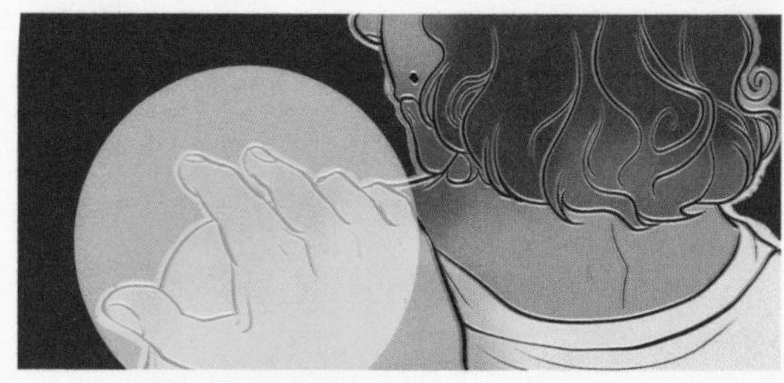

YOU KILLED HIM!

Why didn't you work it out?
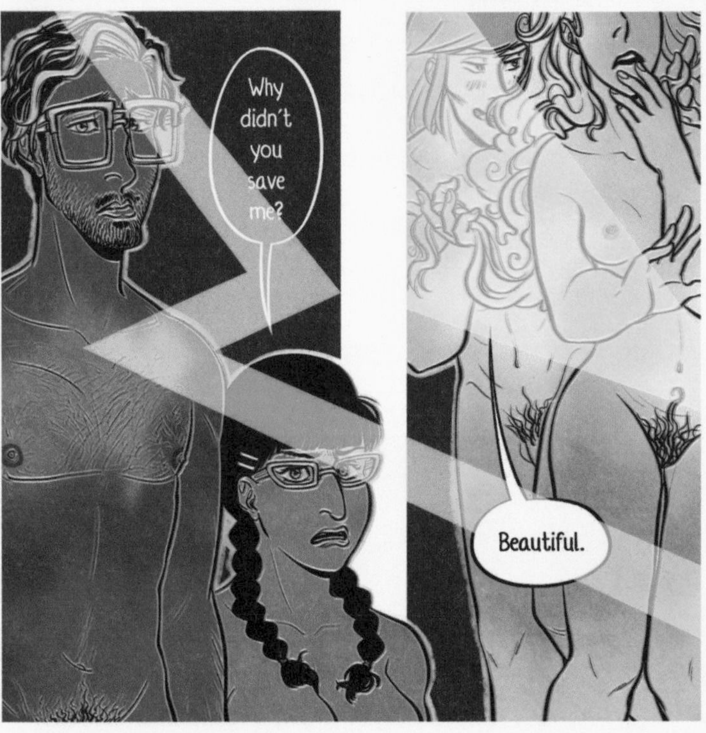
Why didn't you save me?
Beautiful.

You are SO beautiful.

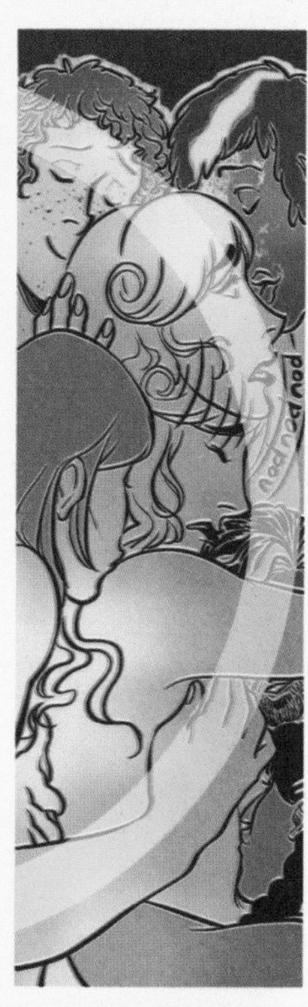

Don't you love ME?

Don't you love ME?

Don't you love ME?

You can't love them all.

toss
toss
LET HE WHO IS WITHOUT SIN...
CAST THE FIRST STONE!
Marie!
MARIE!
Marie!
MARIE!
mAriE--
MARie...!
marie
Mum!

blink
blink
Mum! You're awake!
Are you alright?
Should I—?
You're okay...
DON'T EVEN THINK ABOUT BOTHERING THE NURSES
Yeah, Mum. I'm alright.
Thank God!
WASH YOUR HANDS
Technically,
I wasn't in major danger anyway.
It wasn't a 'real' firework.
Might've just burnt my shoe or something.
Oh...
Well, that's a relief.
...
...
Don't... um...

I didn't mean it. When I said 'leave me alone'.
Well, I did, but...

Just... don't leave me alone like that ever again.
I might want you to leave me alone SOMETIMES but don't actually LEAVE me ALONE.

I know this is a bit hard to grasp but...
It is.

It's just you're a bit much sometimes, so I need some space, but that doesn't mean I don't want you there and...

God, I know this is hard for you to understand—
but—

But I'll try.

Now then.
How long are you going to hang about out there?
Come in here so I can have a proper go at you, Scarpa.

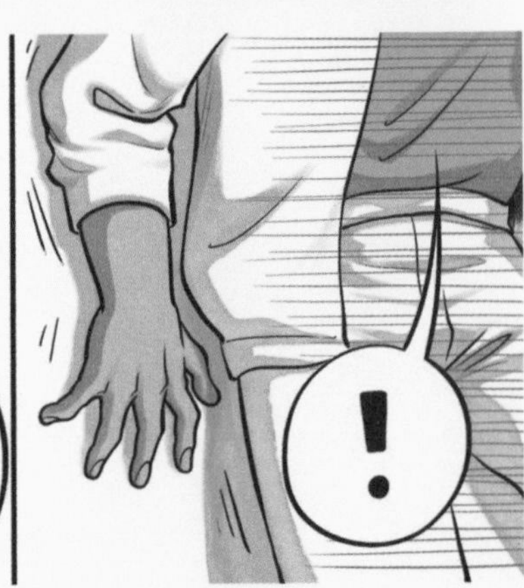

!

← ACCIDENT & EMERGENCY
MAIN ENTRANCE →
X-RAY
Marco?
Miss Lovitt,
er, both of you that is,
um, I'm...

I'm reeeeeaaally sorry!
What the bloody hell is wrong with you?
It wasn't me!

But...
I suppose that doesn't excuse it.

I really am sorry, Miss Lovitt.
I should have stopped Harry the second he got out that firework, then maybe this wouldn't have happened.
But I didn't. They—

WE didn't mean to hurt anyone, we just wanted to...
Look I'm just really, REALLY sorry.

Alright then!

Whaaa? But he—!
He didn't mean to hurt anyone. You heard him.
Okayyy.
Excuse us, hello?
Oh, hello! Come in!
We brought our sons to apologise.
You as well, huh?
Well, go on then!
....sorry.
It's not like WE stabbed her!

It's alright—
Weeeell, that's that.

Boys will be boys and all that, eh?
We'd best be off now.

Uh, Miss Lovitt, about last week—
Come ON, Dad, we're goin' now!

Some things never change.
Wow, what a pair of...
I'm glad I raised you to behave better, Marco.

Are you going to have a proper go at me now too, Miss Lovitt?
Why would she...?

Er, miss, this is my mum—

ENCY
ANCE →
-RAY →
Agnes.

Annie...
Er, yeah.
Did Will bring you here?
He just went to get a tea from the caf.
gulp
Could you go and find him, please?
Oh... kay.
Why don't you go with her, Marco?
Uh, okay.

You can blink, y'know. I'm not goin' anywhere.

I dunno...
You disappeared on me last time I looked away!

. . .

H-how have you... been?
How was the, er, the laundry, wasn't it?
It was...
difficult.
What's with the umbrella?
Oh! Annie must have left it there.
Looks like she cleaned the blood off...
Annie. Your daughter?

?
I haven't been Agnes Ratti since '68.
I'm sorry.
I'm not.
After... the laundry closed in '66...
I met someone... and... well, it gets...
complicated after that.
Suffice to say he buggered off a while ago.
But wait... I've been Marco's form tutor for 5 years now...
He must've told you my name on countless occasions...
He did.
You never came to any parents' evenings either...
No.

Why didn't you—?
I was AFRAID, Marie.

SLUMP
I was so afraid to see you again, I—
I didn't WANT to see you.

Agnes—
The laundry was a fucking horrible place.
I blamed you for me ending up there for a long time.

N-not that I blame you any more, of course!
I know it wasn't your fault.

I just...
sniff
was really angry
...and you weren't there.

I've had a while to get over what happened, Marie.
It's done with now, I don't think about it.
But I've thought about you.
I've thought about you a lot and—
I've missed you.
There's a lot I still want to tell you,
but I don't think I'm ready yet.
When I am, though... will you listen to me, Marie?
Oh, Agnes. I'll always listen to you.

!
Hey, Mum, I brought Will—
So I hear you're awake at last, Sleeping Beau—!
Oh, for the love of—
I leave you alone for five minutes and you're all over some stranger, Marie?

She's no stranger, Will!
Still breaking all the rules, I see, Willie.

RATTY?!

OH MY GOD!
Why didn't you tell me your mum's ex-girlfriend was here, Annie?!

EX...
GIRLFRIEND?

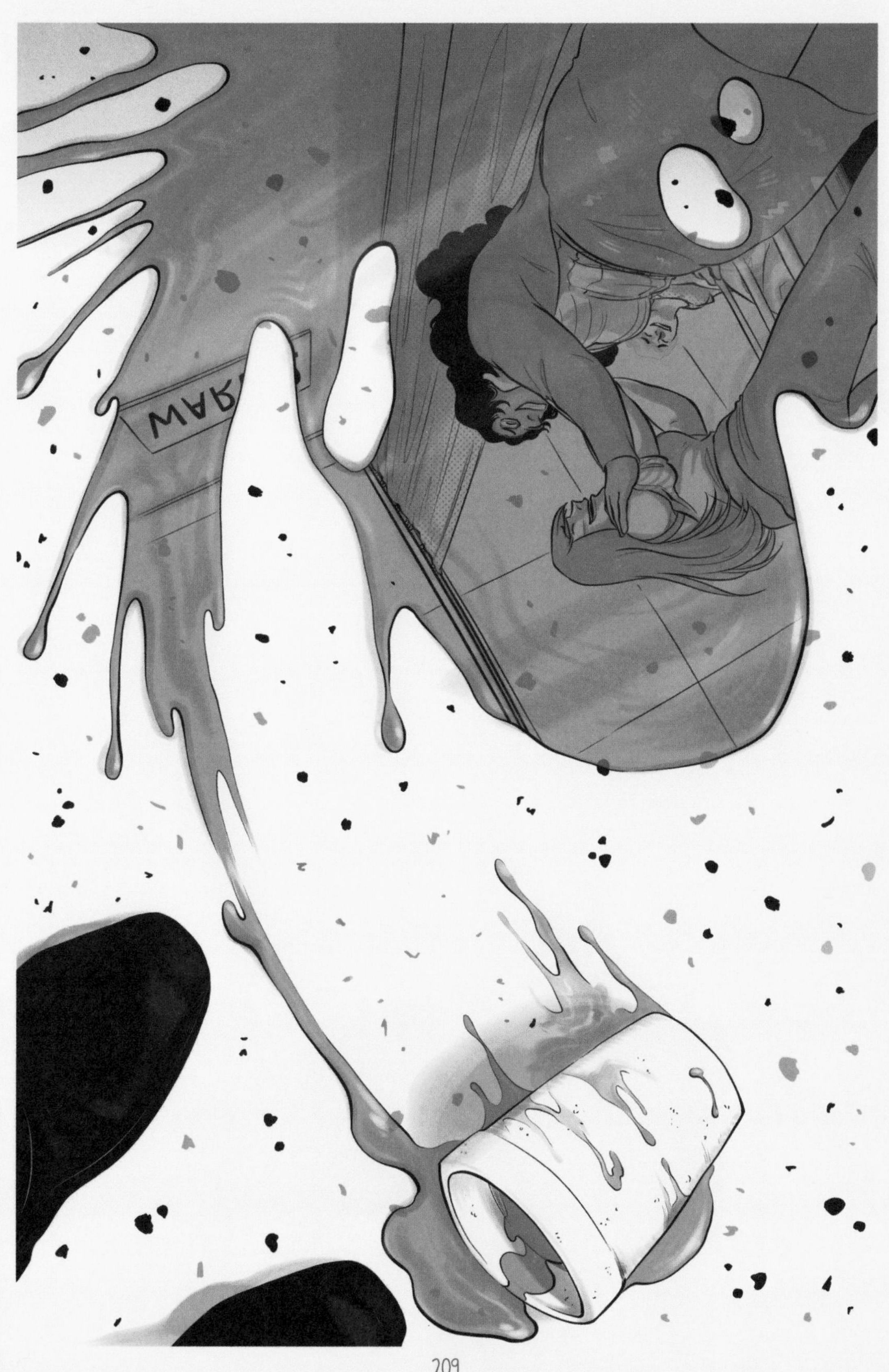

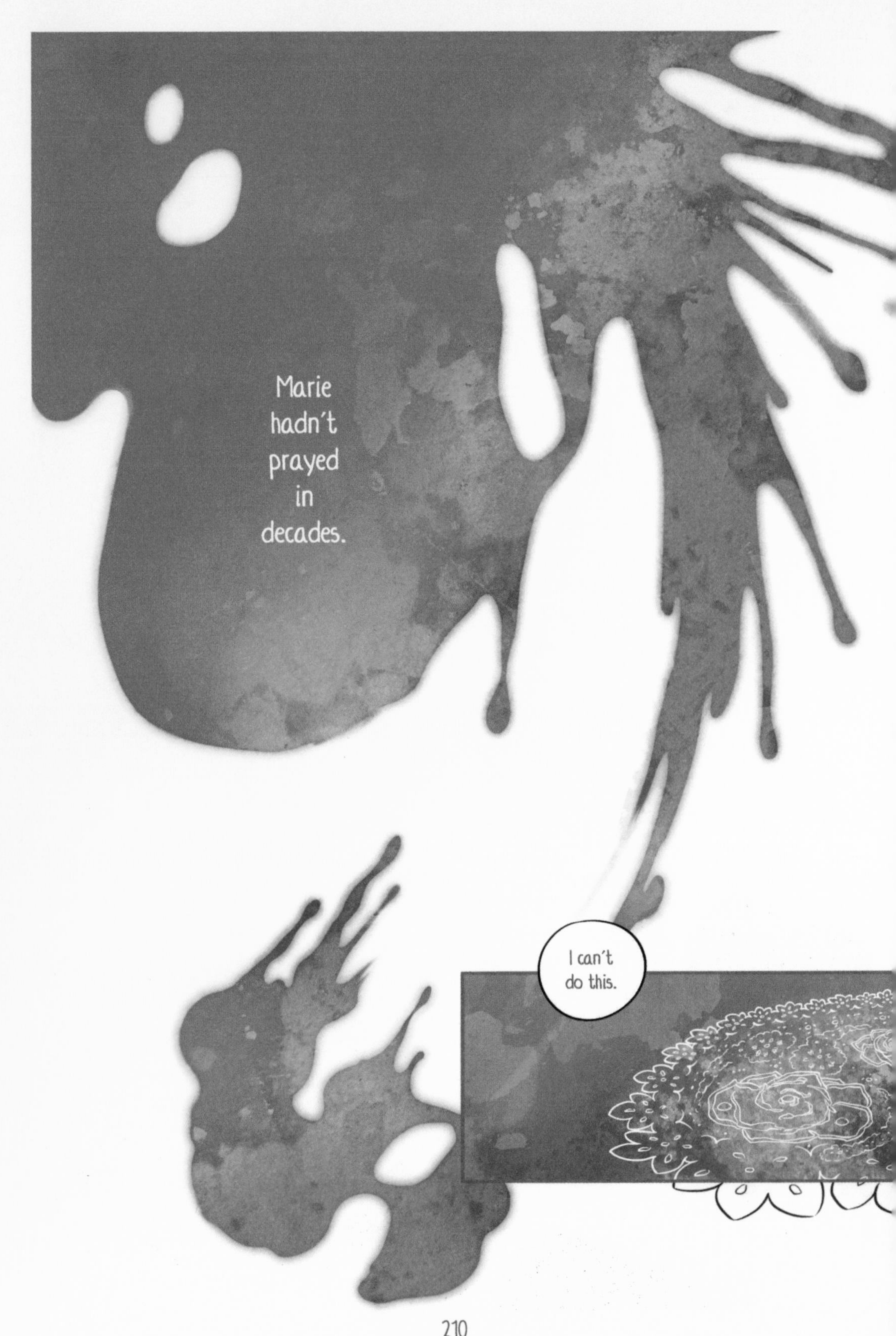
Marie hadn't prayed in decades.
I can't do this.

I can't do this!
I can't do this...
Yes you can.

Mum!
I can't!
How am I supposed to love someone for the rest of my life?!
How do I know my heart won't change?
I can't do this!
The wedding's off, I gotta tell 'em it's...
off!
sit.
Finished?
nod nod
You can't know you're going to love him for ever, it's true.
What?
Then how am I supposed to—
Faith.

I thought you weren't religious anymore.
But that's not what I'm talking about.
I mean you have to have faith that it will all work out.
That you'll still be laughing at his jokes in ten...
If you haven't noticed, we're sitting in a church right now, darling.
twenty...
...maybe fifty years!
...
SNRK
His jokes are AWFUL.
HA! HA HA
Yet here you are, laughing anyway.

Did you laugh at my dad's jokes?
Of course.
But you laugh at Agnes's jokes now, right?
Agnes isn't really the joking type, dear.
You know what I mean.
How can you tell me what love is when your idea of it is so...
confusing?
I've loved a lot of people, Annie.
And every person I've ever loved...
has had an effect on me.

They thought I was the one having an effect on them, but...
They've been the ones helping ME all along.
They've all changed me, and made me into the person I am today.
A better person.
And they all give me hope that maybe there IS a God...
and that God ISN'T a complete WANKER.
MUM!
SHHH, we're in 'that God's' house!
Oh nooo!
Pfff—
Hahahahahahaha

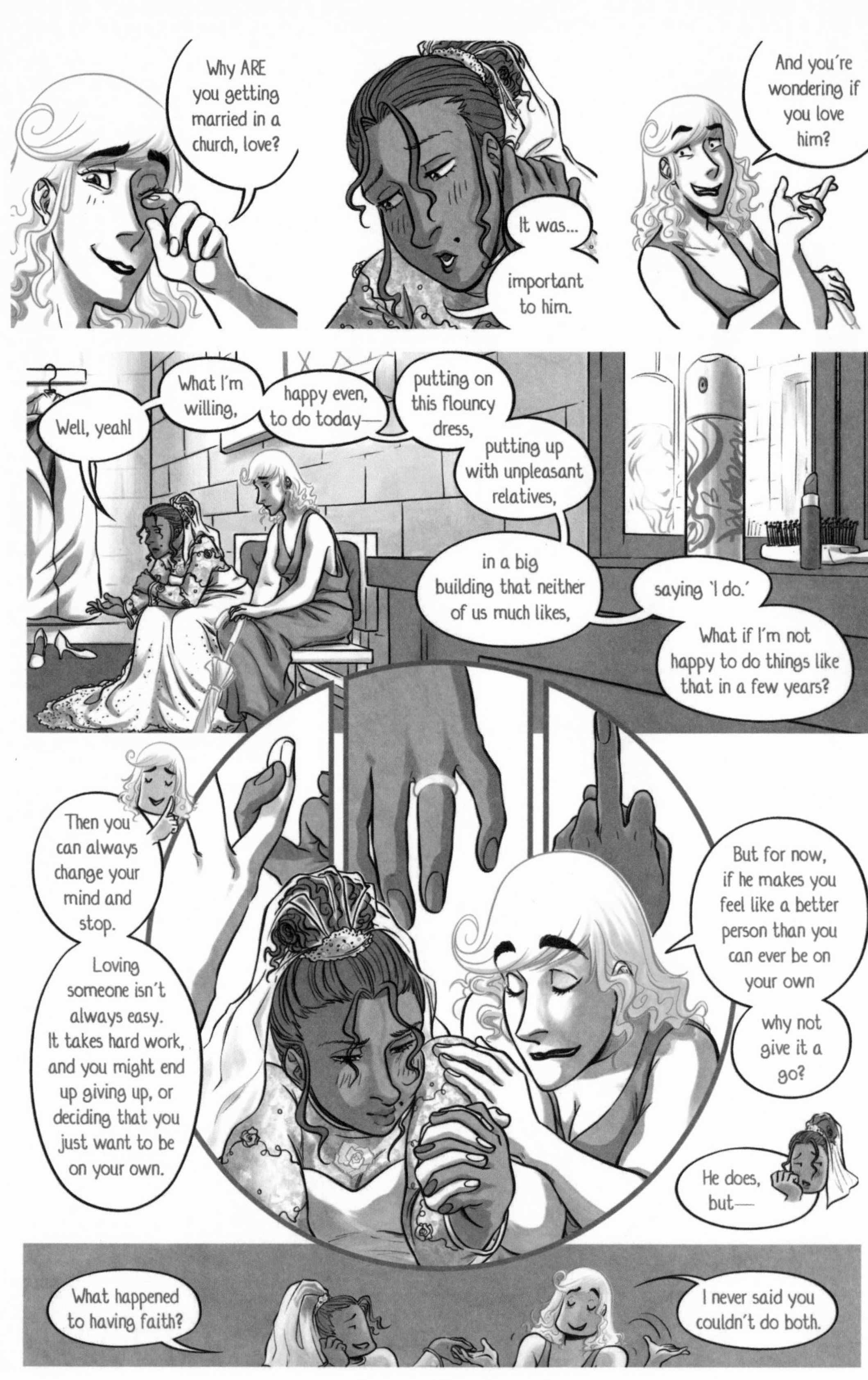
Why ARE you getting married in a church, love?
It was...
important to him.
And you're wondering if you love him?
Well, yeah!
What I'm willing,
happy even, to do today—
putting on this flouncy dress,
putting up with unpleasant relatives,
in a big building that neither of us much likes,
saying 'I do.'
What if I'm not happy to do things like that in a few years?
Then you can always change your mind and stop.
Loving someone isn't always easy. It takes hard work, and you might end up giving up, or deciding that you just want to be on your own.
But for now, if he makes you feel like a better person than you can ever be on your own
why not give it a go?
He does, but—
What happened to having faith?
I never said you couldn't do both.

I've never understood you.
Yes, you have.
You figured out I was a selfish person a long time ago.
I'm the one who had trouble. I've always TRIED to understand you, dear.
But you've always been special.
Listen. Whatever you do today,
you should do it for yourself, and for him, but no one else.
Do what makes you both happy and...
...well, FUCK everyone else!
That's what I've always done.
I know.
Thanks, Mum.
And then, y'know, later you can fu—
OhmyGodMum.

Everything alright?
Yeah.
It's just nerves. She'll be out in a mo'.

Oh God, remember these hymns?
Pffff! I remember Colin used to bellow that one like a foghorn!

Jesus, I remember this one 'n all...
Are you sure everything's okay, Marie?
Yeah... Yeah. I just keep thinking about everyone who *isn't* here. Sorry.

Ahh stop apologising. Prannath's here, y'know? He'll always be here.
I know, but still, they should be here!
And your mum and Johnny made their feelings *quite* clear on this wedding.

Awful or not, they're Annie's family—
Oh, shush.
WE'RE her family, and we're HERE.

Hm?

step...

Yeah.

I s'pose we are.

Annie got married in 1996.

I do.

She never divorced.

That's not to say there weren't unhappy times.

Marie, hurry up, cab's here!
Annie's already at the club!

DAVID
Coming!

oontz
oontz
oontz
FOOTBA
CLOSED for Private function

Because there always are.

eeee eehhhhhhhhhhhhhh
Macaren

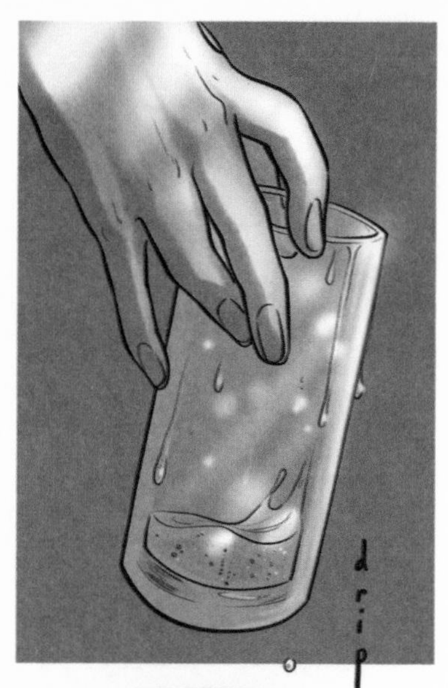
drip....

M IN LOVE WITH YOU MARIE!
plip.

Marie isn't doing ANYTHING she doesn't want to.
You are...
Come on.
Come live with me.
Let's go home
lick
Hey, at leas I'm DEALING with my problems.
I should be the one...
...who looks so beautiful in that dress!
Why don't you prete I'M your husband at your next interview?
Why can't everyone be like YOU, Marie?
guess that means ou're the only woman I'll ever love, Marie!
Awww.
cheers
I'll be here when you get back.

sssSLURP!
CLINK!
But everything is usually alright in the end...
once people kiss and make up.

Grabbed you a glass while I was over there—
Oi, oi, watch it!

You're a TERRIBLE dancer!
You know you love it.

...Yeah.
I do.

She looks so happy.
Mm.
Y'know...
It's funny, I always figured that she'd end up with your Marco.
Guess after all these years I STILL don't quite get her.
What parent ever DOES 'get' their child?
As long as she's happy, that's the main thing.
You're right.
...
I'm sorry, Agnes.
What for?
Ugh.
You're not bringing up the laundry again are you?
I never got to put a ring on your finger.
Oh...
You silly arse.

Don't you remember?

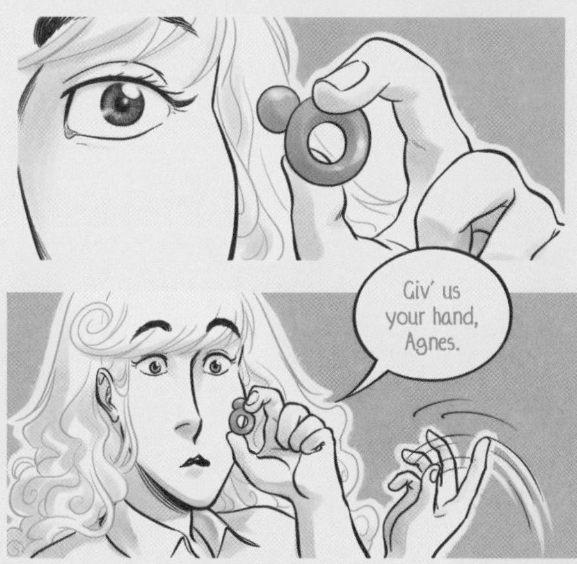

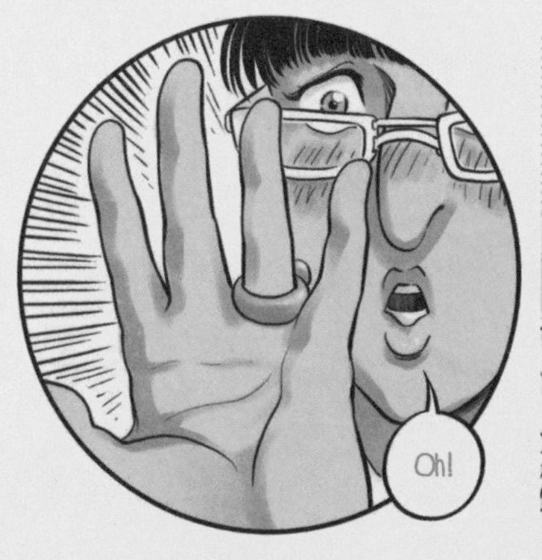

hahahahahaha

I can't believe you remember that!

I still love your stubby fingers.

I know.

Marie hadn't prayed in a long time.

Why is Will...
...snogging my son?
Bwuh—?
BWAHAHAHAHAHA!

She wondered idly if whoever had planned all of this was watching them right now.
Maybe God
or the Fates
Buddha
or Vishnu
Odin
Allah
Amaterasu
or Ptah...
turn

...or even
a comic
artist.
Did they
plan her life up
until this happy
moment?

Did her choices matter...
...gonna be a- a teacher!
FUCK YOU!
...or not?
I'll—
I'LL NEVER
FORGIVE YOU!
Is there a Heaven
or a Hell, that our choices land us in?
Marie?

Marie could have thought about this
Hm?
?
and got a bit depressed.
(As certain people are wont to do at parties like these.)
But instead
she grabbed another drink
twirled with Agnes
and enjoyed herself.
Your mum's fun.
Yeah.
Fuck that.

It doesn't matter in the end, all that matters in life is—
Mm!
Marie, I'm trying to end the book on a poignant—
Shhh. I'm trying to kiss my girlfriend!
Oh for the love of...
The End

ACKNOWLEDGEMENTS

THANK YOU TO **MUM**, **DAD** AND **DANIEL**, FOR LETTING ME GRUMBLE AROUND THE HOUSE FOR THE YEAR IT TOOK TO MAKE THIS SEXY BOOK, AND FOR KEEPING MY TEA LEVELS STABLE.

I KNOW YOU STILL FEEL GUILTY ABOUT IT, BUT THANKS, **MUM**, FOR SENDING ME TO CATHOLIC SCHOOL AND THAT ONE CATHOLIC SUMMER CAMP. I HATED THEM BUT IF YOU HADN'T DONE IT I WOULDN'T BE WHO I AM TODAY, AND I WOULDN'T HAVE HAD THE IDEA FOR MARIE!

THANKS TO **ALL MY FRIENDS** WHO'VE HELPED HERE AND THERE WITH ADVICE ON THE STORY AND ART, WHO'VE KEPT ME GOING WHEN I'VE HAD DOUBTS. WITHOUT YOU THIS BOOK MIGHT'VE BEEN WAY LESS SMUTTY.
SPECIAL THANKS HERE TO **NIN** FOR TELLING ME I DRAW A NICE VULVA (AMONG OTHER THINGS).

THANKS TO THE JUDGES OF THE FIRST GRAPHIC NOVEL COMPETITION 2014 – **ANDY**, **NICOLA**, **WOODROW**, **MEG** AND **CORINNE** – FOR CHOOSING MARIE AS YOUR WINNER. WITHOUT YOU, MYRIAD WOULD NEVER HAVE SEEN MARIE.

AND THANKS TO **MYRIAD EDITIONS**, MY EDITOR **CORINNE** AND THE STAFF, FOR PUBLISHING THIS RISQUÉ BOOK AND HANDLING MY DEMANDING NATURE WHEN IT CAME TO EDITING AND PRINTING IT. I JUST HAVE A LOT OF FEELINGS ABOUT COMICS AND PAPER. SENSUAL FEELINGS.
EXTRA THANKS AGAIN TO **WOODROW** FOR HIS HELP WITH LAYOUTS, AND **EMMA** FOR HER HELP WITH DIALOGUE.

FINALLY, THANK YOU TO MY EXECUTIVE PRODUCER, BEST BOY AND FETCHING LIFE MODEL: **DEAN**.
WITHOUT YOU I WOULDN'T REALLY UNDERSTAND... FEELINGS, AND THEREFORE WOULDN'T HAVE CREATED MARIE AS SHE IS NOW.
ALSO THANKS FOR YOUR ADVICE ON DRAWING DICKS, THAT WAS HELPFUL TOO.

More comics by Jade Sarson,
creator of
For the Love of God, Marie!
Cafe
SUADA
The comic with tea leaves, coffee beans & a dash of romance!
Down by the riverside there is a quaint little teahouse run by our heroine, Geraldine, whose only desire is to spread her love of the golden beverage - But what's going to happen to her business when a new coffeehouse springs up right *NEXT DOOR?!*
Nominated in 2013 for the British Comic Awards for Best Emerging Talent, *Cafe Suada* is a battle of the beverages that will leave you thirsty for more than just a cup of tea!

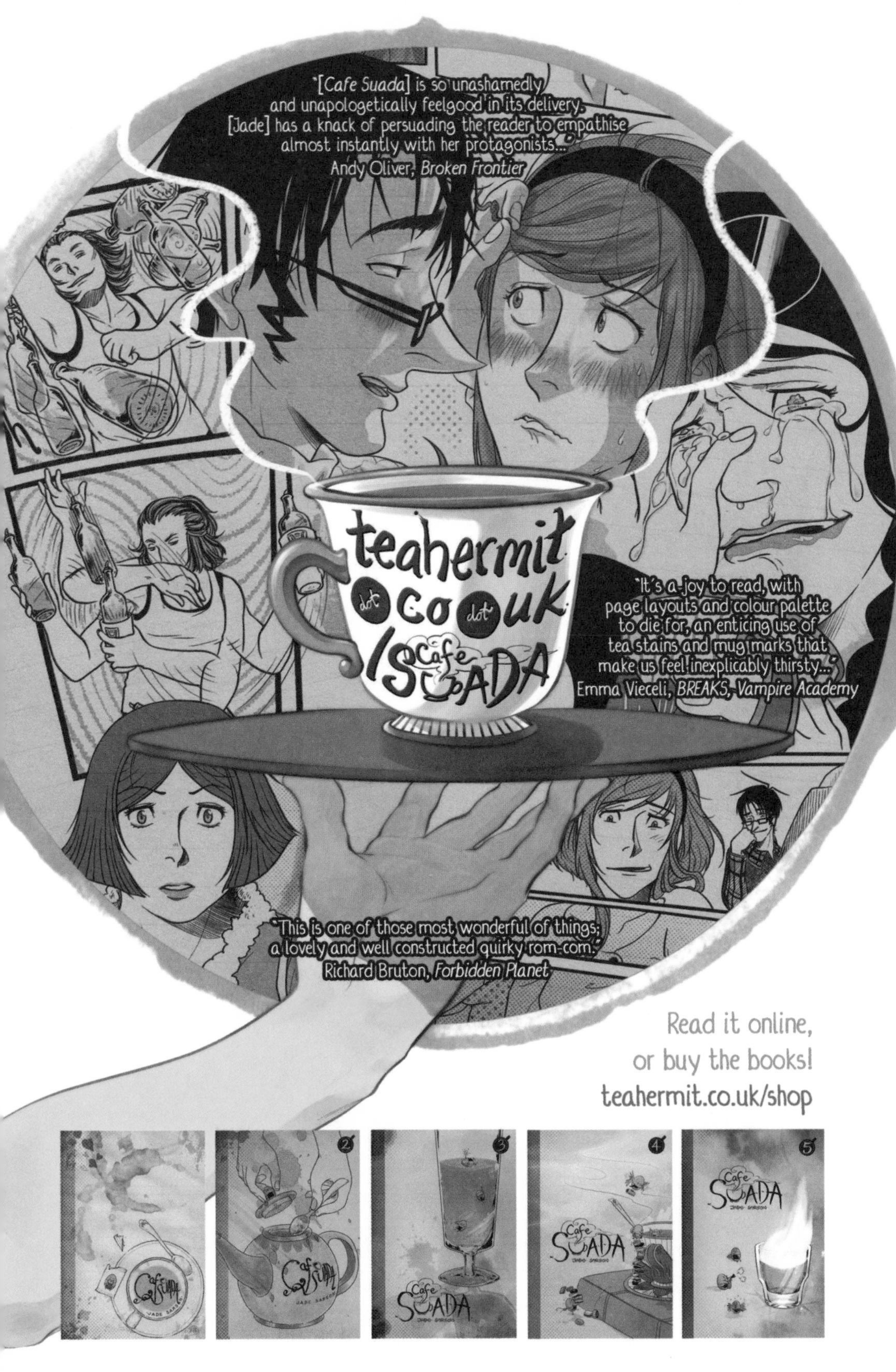
"[Cafe Suada] is so unashamedly and unapologetically feelgood in its delivery. [Jade] has a knack of persuading the reader to empathise almost instantly with her protagonists..."
Andy Oliver, Broken Frontier
teahermit dot co dot uk
is Cafe Suada
"It's a joy to read, with page layouts and colour palette to die for, an enticing use of tea stains and mug marks that make us feel inexplicably thirsty..."
Emma Vieceli, BREAKS, Vampire Academy
"This is one of those most wonderful of things; a lovely and well constructed quirky rom-com."
Richard Bruton, Forbidden Planet
Read it online,
or buy the books!
teahermit.co.uk/shop

MORE FROM MYRIAD

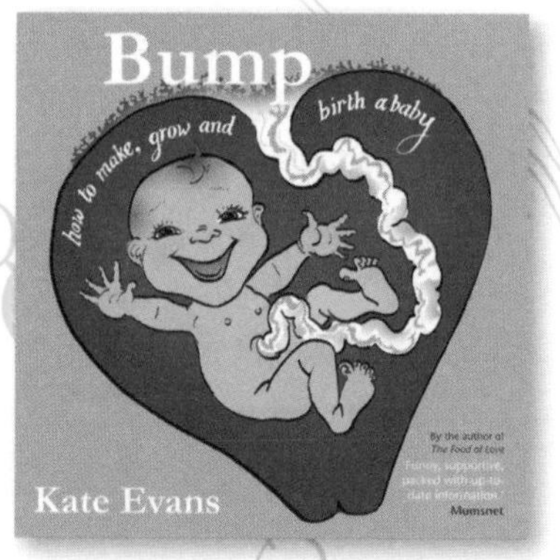

MYRIAD FIRST GRAPHIC NOVEL COMPETITION

WINNER 2012

WINNER 2014

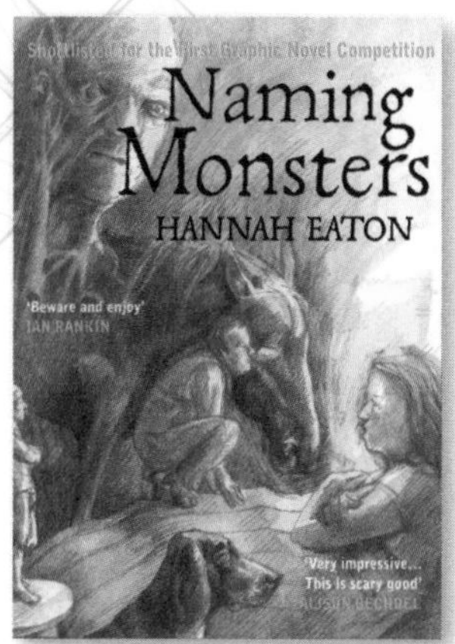

SHORTLISTED 2012

SHORTLISTED 2012

SHORTLISTED 2012

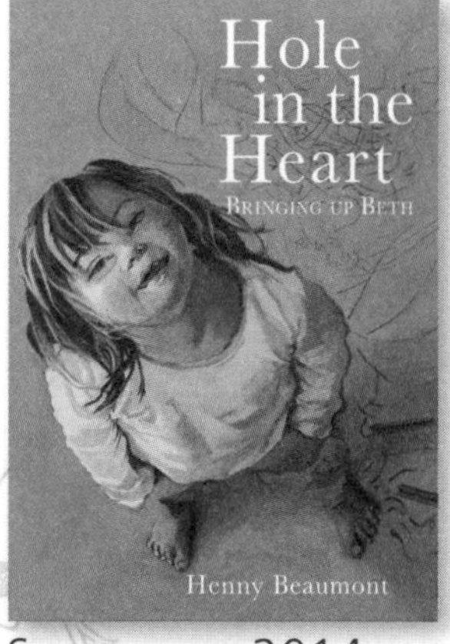

SHORTLISTED 2014

Sign up to our mailing list at

www.myriadeditions.com

Follow us on Facebook and Twitter